The Wild Shores of
Patagonia

The Wild Shores of
Patagonia

The Valdés Peninsula
& Punta Tombo

Text and Photographs by
Jasmine Rossi

Foreword by William Conway

Harry N. Abrams, Inc., Publishers

To my mother,
who always encouraged me to pursue my dreams.

PAGES 2–3: *Orcas swimming along the banks of Caleta Valdés.*
PAGES 4–5: *The shoreline of the Valdés Peninsula.*
PAGES 6–7: *Six little sea lion pups return from playing in the pools formed by the outgoing tide.*

Excerpt from "The Wellfleet Whale" © 1983 by Stanley Kunitz. All rights reserved. Published by Sheep Meadow Press, New York. Reprinted by permission of the author.

PROJECT COORDINATION: *Dudu von Thielmann*
DESIGN: *Molly Shields*

First published in 2000 by Ediciones Larivière, Buenos Aires

Published in 2000 by Harry N. Abrams, Incorporated, New York

Printed and bound in Italy by Mondadori Printing

LIBRARY OF CONGRESS CATALOGING-IN-PUBLICATION DATA
Rossi, Jasmine.
    The wild shores of Patagonia : The Valdés Peninsula and Punta Tombo / Jasmine Rossi ;
    foreword by William Conway
        p. cm.
    Includes bibliographical references (p.).
    ISBN 0-8109-4352-2
        1. Zoology–Patagonia (Argentina and Chile) 2. Zoology–Patagonia (Argentina and Chile)–Pictorial works. I. Title.
QL239 .R67 2000
591.982'74'0222-dc21   00-29289

Harry N. Abrams, Inc.
100 Fifth Avenue
New York, N.Y. 10011
www.abramsbooks.com

Contents

FOREWORD

*C*rashing and swirling on puntas and peninsulas and seething up great shingle beaches in twenty-foot tides, the cold Malvinas current washes Patagonia's harsh shores. It carries vast schools of plankton and fishes, squids and shrimps, and it nurtures spectacular aggregations of sea lions and elephant seals, colonies of penguins and cormorants, and pods of right whales and orcas. Ancient and robust, the coast's wildlife is a broken and knotted band of biodiversity, with 150 colonies of sea birds and 75 colonies of seals and sea lions, scattered far apart along the shore of some 2,000 miles (3,000 km). Their distant spacing emphasizes both the tentative nature of their resources and the newly fragile status of their future.

Diving over three thousand feet (over 1,000 m) into the oceanic abyss at the edge of the Patagonian shelf, the world's largest seals hunt bioluminescent fishes and squids far from their Valdés breeding colonies. Hour after hour, month after month, female elephant seals hunt to accumulate the nutrients required to produce and nurture their pups, while males seek to build the strength they will need to compete with other males for harems of females. But recently they and the big southern sea lions have been facing tough competition with the huge oceanic vessels that were specially constructed to fish the same rough waters for those same foods. Patagonia's coastal creatures cast a spell that is both brusque and elemental. The lonely coasts, incessant winds, huge mammals, and hardy birds are austere and awesome.

The center of this coastal life zone is the Valdés Peninsula in the province of Chubut. There, photojournalist Jasmine Rossi lived for almost two years, capturing in pictures its magnificent vistas and imposing wildlife—orcas, penguins, elephant seals.

Rossi's extraordinary photographs show the great male elephant seals at war and females and pups at the moment of birth. They reveal the gleaming beauty of the killer whales that hunt sea lions and the dramatic horrors of their bloody success. These images carry us back to an undisturbed and previous age, but all of these powerful animals are captives of the rich and uninterrupted bounty of the cold ocean currents sweeping north from Antarctica.

Every creature that breeds upon the coast's barren shore has always competed with others for reproductive rights, space, and food. Orcas eat sea lions; sea lions may eat penguins. Today, however, these creatures face growing competition in their primeval waters from the world's fastest-growing fishery. Although right whales, sea lions, elephant seals, fur seals, cormorants, and even penguins have been hunted by man on the shores of Patagonia since ancient peoples camped there 10,000 years ago, recent escalations in fishing indicate that we are facing the total and irreparable loss of this important natural treasure.

By fortuitous accident, Rossi spent a short leave from her job with the European Parliament in London to travel in South America, where she was captivated by the beauty of its wildernesses. She was so inspired by the dramas that unfolded before her eyes that even though she did not have a significant photo credit to her name, she set out to do a picture book of this complex and troubled scene. Focusing her exceptional talents, she was determined to convey to others her own appreciation of what she had seen. After seeking guidance from photographers and publishers, she moved to the Valdés Peninsula to begin her project.

Rossi's spectacular photographs of Patagonia's coastal wild animals and seascapes are beautiful and shocking. She portrays its cycles of birth and death, storm and calm, with rare technical skill and a text that enlarges her photographic windows with unusual accuracy. Her book is a passionate contribution to the growing campaign of those working to protect the wildlife of Patagonia.

Even as this volume goes to press, word has come that the province of Chubut is considering oil drilling and derrick construction along the shores of the Valdés Peninsula, right among this unique wildlife and amid these extraordinary vistas. It is now necessary to contemplate a time when greed and ignorance might make this album one of the last records of a coastal Eden whose likes can be found nowhere else on earth.

William Conway
Senior Conservationist,
Wildlife Conservation Society

Above: TWO-THIRDS OF THE 30,000 SOUTH AMERICAN SEA LIONS THAT LIVE ALONG THE COASTS OF NORTHERN PATAGONIA ARE FOUND AT THE VALDÉS PENINSULA.

Right: LOW TIDE EXPOSES THE BROAD PROTECTIVE REEFS THAT SHIELD THE CALETA VALDÉS ELEPHANT SEAL ROOKERY FROM THE CRASHING WAVES OF THE OPEN SOUTH ATLANTIC AND FROM AMBUSH ATTACKS BY HUNGRY ORCAS.

Page 8: THE MAGELLANIC PENGUIN MAY MIGRATE MORE THAN 3,700 MILES (6,000 KM) DURING ITS ANNUAL ROUND TRIP BETWEEN ITS BRAZILIAN FEEDING GROUNDS AND ITS PATAGONIAN BREEDING COLONIES.

Sanctuary at the End of the World

*P*atagonia is a vast region that extends from the Pacific to the Atlantic oceans, and from the Rio Negro, which makes its northern boundary, to Tierra del Fuego, the triangular island at its southernmost tip. Over twice the size of California, Patagonia spreads across some 350,000 square miles (900,000 sq. km) and straddles two countries, Chile and Argentina.

Since the time of its first European settlers, Patagonia's austere resources have ensured it to be a place for only the stouthearted. Although Magellan's expedition of 1520 passed along the coasts of the Valdés Peninsula, it was not until the late eighteenth century that Spanish explorers discovered the peninsula's valuable salt beds, which they began to mine in 1784. That same year, Don Francisco de Medina was granted a whaling license, and he killed over fifty of these gentle giants without ever leaving the Gulf of San José. In 1810, all but five of the fifty men in the San José settlement were massacred, and the rest driven out, by the native Tehuelche Indians. It would be another seventy-two years before the next settlers returned. Today, Emilio Jorge Ferro, a descendant of

those late-nineteenth-century settlers, still runs a 272,000-acre (110,000-ha) sheep farm that covers nearly one third of the peninsula—nowadays, sheep farming is the peninsula's only commercial industry.

In the nineteenth century the peninsula's seas became a destination for whalers, and over seven hundred whaling ships patrolled the waters. The last commercial exploitation was sea lion hunting, which began in 1914 and lasted until 1953.

Patagonia is a land of extremes: it is home to some of the world's most challenging summits, immense continental ice fields, and vast desert plains. More than anything, Patagonia is the land of the wind. The region lies between the thirty-ninth and fifty-sixth parallels, for which plighted mariners have nicknamed its treacherous oceans the "roaring forties" and "raging fifties," referring to the ceaseless gales that plague South America's tail end.

Originating in the Pacific Ocean, the wind blows east across the towering Andes, down lush alpine meadows and over vast open plains, often reaching speeds in excess of sixty miles (100 km) per hour. As

SOUTH AMERICA REACHES FARTHER TOWARD THE SOUTH POLE THAN ANY OTHER CONTINENTAL LAND MASS—MANY PEOPLE ARE SURPRISED TO LEARN THAT THE CITY OF CAPE TOWN LIES FARTHER NORTH THAN BUENOS AIRES. FORMING THE LAST, TAPERING SEGMENT OF SOUTH AMERICA, PATAGONIA IS KNOWN AS THE "UTTERMOST PART OF THE EARTH."

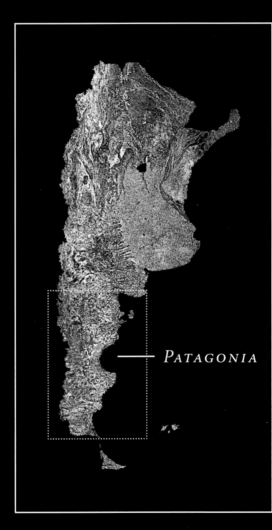

PENÍNSULA VALDÉS

PUNTA TOMBO

PATAGONIA

ARGENTINA

PATAGONIA

GOLFO SAN MATÍAS

GOLFO SAN JOSÉ

Punta Norte

Punta Buenos Aires

Caleta Valdés

El Salitral
-52 ft. (-16 m)

Isla de los Pájaros

Riacho San José

Caleta Valdés Ranger's Station

Punta Pirámide

Puerto Pirámide

Salina Grande
-157 ft. (-48 m)

Punta Hercules

GOLFO NUEVO

Salina Chica
-115 ft. (-35 m)

Puerto Madryn

Punta Delgada

Punta Loma

Punta Ninfas

warm air collides with icy peaks, snow and rain fall heavily, and almost all moisture is lost to the mountains and adjacent valleys. Less than eight inches (200 mm) of annual rainfall are left for the sweeping eastern steppe—a desolate desert of gravel; parched yellow grasses; and low, drab bushes. Here the arid plain levels out until it drops abruptly into the Atlantic. To the northeast, the Valdés Peninsula juts out into the ocean like a gigantic mushroom, and is connected to the Argentine mainland by an isthmus so narrow the sea is visible on either side. The 1400-square-mile (3,625-sq.-km) peninsula is about the size of the state of Rhode Island, and encompasses two almost land-locked gulfs, the Gulf of San José to the north, and the New Gulf (Golfo Nuevo) to the south. Like the arid

desert plains, the Valdés Peninsula lies in the rain shadow of the Andes, although the maritime climate is slightly more benign here than farther inland.

Flat and treeless, the peninsula's landscape is marked by stark, mesa-like plains thinly covered with a scrubland of thorny thickets that stretches as far as the eye can see. Yet, what appears empty and monotonous at first sight harbors many natural wonders. Two large salt flats, which lie in the middle of the peninsula, are testimony to former incursions of the sea. The smaller, Salina Chica, lies at 115 feet (35 m) below sea level, and the larger, Salina Grande, at 157 feet (48 m) below sea level. The fourteen-square-mile (35-sq.-km) Salina Grande is the lowest point on the South American continent—on earth, it is third only in

depth to the Dead Sea and North America's Death Valley. But just offshore, in the center of the New Gulf, lie some of the deepest waters on Argentina's continental shelf. Where the arid steppe meets the sea, rolling dunes of sand reaching the height of a multi-storied building alternate with sheer, 260-foot (80-m) cliffs that break abruptly into the ocean.

The peninsula's tides are enormous—with a difference of up to thirty-three feet (10 m) between high and low tide, a range second only in the world to those of Nova Scotia's Bay of Fundy. This generates violent currents, which at the narrow mouths of the Caleta Valdés inlet and of the two almost landlocked gulfs, can reach speeds in excess of six knots—strong enough to sweep adult right whales onto the sand banks at the Caleta's entrance.

Flint arrowheads from the extinct Tehuelche Indians, who had formerly inhabited the area, litter the plains. All along the coast, plate-sized, fossilized oysters, tens of millions of years old, speckle the sedimentary rocks that form the ancient seabed. In fact,

there are so many thousands of enormous fossilized oysters and sea shells that it is impossible in some areas to reach the shore without stepping on them.

The Valdés Peninsula and Punta Tombo—the two-mile- (3-km-) long headland that juts into the ocean 155 miles (250 km) south of the peninsula—attract astonishing concentrations of marine mammals and birds. The peninsula's inlets, bays, and sheltered gulfs are a vast natural refuge for many species escaping Patagonia's bleak shoreline and dangerous winds. Along some 3,000 miles (5,000 km) of rugged shores, no other place hosts more formidable concentrations of marine mammals and birds than the Valdés Peninsula and Punta Tombo. Almost a third of the southern right whale population regularly visits the peninsula's gulfs to breed and bear their young, while Punta Tombo is home to the world's largest continental penguin rookery. Inscribed by the United Nations as a World Heritage site in 1999, the Valdés Peninsula is one of the most ecologically fascinating regions, and one of the last truly wild places on earth.

OVER 100,000 SHEEP GRAZE ON THE VALDÉS PENINSULA. THEY DRINK BRACKISH WATER THAT IS PUMPED TO THE SURFACE BY WINDMILLS. THE ONLY FRESHWATER SPRINGS ON THE ENTIRE PENINSULA LIE AT THE SOUTH END OF THE SALINA GRANDE SALT FLAT, WHERE THE ARID STEPPE SUDDENLY TURNS INTO LUSH, GREEN PASTURE.

Part 1
A South Atlantic Nursery

No wind. No waves. No clouds.
    Only the whisper of the tide,
      as it withdrew, stroking the shore,
a lazy drift of gulls overhead,
    and tiny points of light
      bubbling in the channel.
It was the tag-end of summer.
    From the harbor's mouth
      you coasted into sight,
flashing news of your advent,
    the crescent of your dorsal fin
      clipping the diamonded surface.
We cheered at the sign of your greatness
    when the black barrel of your head
      erupted, ramming the water,
and you flowered for us
    in the jet of your spouting.

All afternoon you swam
    tirelessly round the bay,
      with such an easy motion,
the slightest downbeat of your tail,
    an almost imperceptible
      undulation of your flippers,
you seemed like something poured,
    not driven; you seemed
      to marry grace with power.
And when you bounded into air,
    slapping your flukes,
      we thrilled to look upon
pure energy incarnate
    as nobility of form.
      You seemed to ask of us
not sympathy, or love,
    or understanding,
      but awe and wonder.

STANLEY KUNITZ
"The Wellfleet Whale"

Chapter One
Mammals of the Southern Seas

Page 19: THE SHORE OF THE NEW GULF.

Opposite: IN 1977 AN ORCA NAMED MEL, PUNTA NORTE'S ASSIDUOUS HUNTER, WAS SHOT AT PUNTA BERMEJA, NORTH OF THE VALDÉS PENINSULA. MEL SWAM TO SAFETY, BUT HIS CROOKED DORSAL FIN STILL BEARS TESTIMONY TO A BULLET WOUND.

Right: ONE OF A SMALL GROUP OF RISSO'S DOLPHINS THAT REGULARLY VISITS THE GULF OF SAN JOSÉ. RISSO'S DOLPHINS CAN GROW TO NEARLY THIRTEEN FEET (4 M) IN LENGTH, AND HAVE EXCEPTIONALLY TALL, CONCAVE DORSAL FINS THAT, WHEN SEEN FROM AFAR, ARE EASY TO CONFUSE WITH THOSE OF FEMALE AND JUVENILE ORCAS. FROM UP CLOSE THEY HAVE A RATHER TAT-TERED APPEARANCE: THEIR GRAYISH BODIES ARE COVERED WITH RAKE MARKS INFLICTED BY OTHER RISSO'S DOLPHINS, AND SCARS FROM CONFRONTATIONS WITH THEIR FAVORITE PREY, DEEP-WATER SQUID. AS THEY GROW OLDER, THEIR LEAD-GRAY COATS FADE TO SILVER AND SOMETIMES TURN ALMOST WHITE.

*I*n contrast to the barren land along its shores, the South Atlantic ocean is bountiful. Fed by the nutrient-rich Malvinas current that sweeps cold Antarctic waters across one of the world's broadest continental shelves, Patagonia's seas support one of the richest marine faunas in the world. Vast amounts of plankton and algae, crustaceans, and enormous shoals of bait fish such as the Fuegian sardine and the little anchovy support a complex food chain of larger fishes, birds, and marine mammals, many of which can be found at the Valdés Peninsula.

Almost a third of the southern right whale *(Eubalaena australis)* population regularly visits the peninsula's sheltered gulfs to breed and bear their young. Although the right whale is the most endangered of all large whales, at the height of the breeding season almost 600 whales can be found in the waters surrounding the peninsula. Approximately 43,000 southern elephant seals *(Mirounga leonina),* the largest of all seals in the world, come to the peninsula's open ocean shores to breed and molt. Valdés is their only continental rookery, since they mostly breed on sub-

Antarctic islands. The peninsula is also home to a pod of orcas *(Orcinus orca)* that, at considerable risk to their own lives, have the unusual practice of catapulting themselves through shallow water onto the shore in order to snatch elephant seals, as well as the southern sea lions *(Otaria flavescens)* that haul out by the thousands on the rocks along the coast.

In 1996, a dead Hector's beaked whale *(Mesoplodon hectori)* washed up on the peninsula's shore. It was only the twenty-eighth time this species had ever been sighted—anywhere. Very little is known

about this whale, which until 1975 had only been seen dead, and there are still just two known sightings of a live one. They are about thirteen feet (4 m) long and have many scratches and scars on their bodies, but their dorsal fin is very small. Males have two triangular teeth protruding from the tip of their lower jaw.

Hundreds of acrobatic dusky dolphins *(Lagenorhynchus obscurus)* inhabit the Gulf of San José, where they flaunt their spectacular leaps. Groups of up to one hundred bottlenose dolphins *(Tursiops*

air every three to four minutes, in contrast to bottlenose dolphins, which can stay underwater for up to fifteen minutes at a time.

The Valdés Peninsula lies at the southernmost boundary of the common dolphin's range, but lies at the northernmost limit of the territory of the Commerson's dolphin *(Cephalorhynchus commersonii),* which extends all the way south to Tierra del Fuego. The Commerson's dolphin has a jet-black dorsal fin, snout, flippers, and flukes, but the main part of

truncatus) are occasionally sighted at the Gulf of San José. During the 1970s, researcher Bernd Würsig identified fifty-three individuals that regularly came to the gulf's placid waters. Sadly, sightings have since dropped dramatically, although a core group continues to appear sporadically along the shores.

Common dolphins *(Delphinus delphis),* which have a handsome yellow-gray hourglass pattern on their flanks, occasionally visit the peninsula's waters to forage for anchovies. They are the fastest swimmers among the small dolphins, but they must come up for

its body is snow-white. It breaches frequently and enjoys surfing large waves close to shore.

A pod of large grayish-white Risso's dolphins *(Grampus griseus)* is regularly spotted at the Gulf of San José, although these dolphins normally prefer deeper waters. They have extremely tall dorsal fins that look similar to those of female killer whales.

The black Burmeister's porpoise *(Phocoena spinipinnis)* is also a regular at Valdés. It is one of the most abundant cetaceans in southern South American waters, and comes very close to shore after dark. Only

about half the size of a Risso's dolphin, it is shy and inconspicuous. Unlike Risso's, common, and dusky dolphins, which leap, spyhop, lobtail, and flipperslap, the Burmeister's porpoise rarely indulges in such aquatic acrobatics. Instead, it causes barely a ripple as it surfaces, making it hard to detect.

It is more unusual to see the southern right whale dolphin *(Lissodelphis peronii)* at Valdés, since this animal is generally thought to prefer deeper offshore waters. This is the only dolphin species to live in the southern hemisphere, that has no dorsal fin. All known sightings of Commerson's and southern right whale dolphins at Valdés have occurred at the New Gulf.

Southern Right Whale (*Eubalaena australis*)

IN 1984 THE RIGHT WHALE WAS DECLARED A NATIONAL MONUMENT IN ARGENTINA, WHICH GRANTED THE SPECIES MAXIMUM PROTECTION. ALTHOUGH THE SOUTHERN HEMISPHERE POPULATION NOW GROWS AT OVER 7 PERCENT PER YEAR, THE RIGHT WHALE REMAINS THE RAREST OF ALL LARGE WHALES IN THE WORLD.

RIGHT WHALES ARE ROBUST AND STOCKY. FEMALES ARE SLIGHTLY LARGER THAN MALES, GROWING UP TO SOME FIFTY-FIVE FEET (17 M) AND WEIGHING OVER EIGHTY TONS. THEY HAVE MASSIVE HEADS THAT MAKE UP ALMOST A THIRD OF THEIR BODIES, WITH ENORMOUS, STRONGLY ARCHED JAWS AND LIPS. THEIR SKIN IS BLACK OR DARK GRAY IN COLOR, WITH DISTINCT WHITE MARKINGS ON THEIR BELLIES THAT VARY IN EACH INDIVIDUAL.

The right whale is one of only eleven baleen, or "toothless," species of whales. As they are skim feeders, the whale's bristly baleen—which runs the entire length of its upper jaw—allows it to swim through the water with its mouth agape, filtering the water with this giant strainer. Then, with its muscular tongue the whale licks the plankton, krill, and copepod crustaceans from its baleen.

Right whales have been hunted for this fine, flexible baleen, which was used in the past to make a variety of articles, from umbrella ribs to corsets. They have also been hunted for their valuable blubber, of which they have so much that they float even when dead. As their English name aptly describes, these *were* the "right" whales to hunt.

Their name in Spanish, *ballena franca* (which means "innocent whale") suggests a whale of gentle disposition that was friendly, curious, and approachable. Contrary to most other whales, right whales are exceptionally slow swimmers and have coastal habits. Despite their size and strength, right whales are so docile that unlike other species of whale, they put up little fight, even when brutally butchered.

A Whale Sighting

I was once on an a cruise ship traveling near the island of South Georgia and the Falkland Islands. We came across a solitary right whale. The boat stopped, and soon the whale began circling around the bow. While people bent over the railing and dangled their cameras to capture the astonishing sight, the whale rolled around and around, performing several curious back flips that showed off its mottled black and white belly. It was just a speck in front of a huge ocean liner, completely vulnerable, yet unafraid. Unfortunately, the same disposition that today can delight hordes of tourists has brought these whales to the brink of extinction.

The right whale was once found in abundance along all continents, in both hemispheres. Its thick coat of blubber makes the whale shun the hot waters of the tropical belt between twenty degrees north and south, giving rise to two almost identical but genetically isolated populations: the northern right whale (*Eubalaena glacialis*) and the southern right whale (*Eubalaena australis*).

The southern right whale inhabits the circumpo-

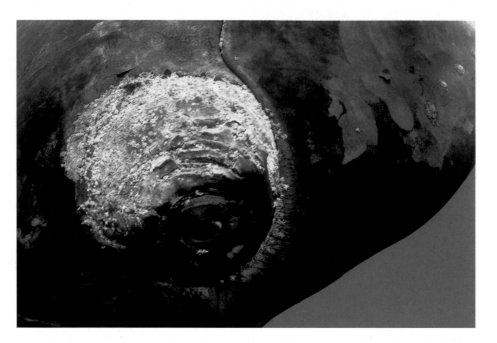

lar waters of the southern hemisphere up to sixty-four degrees south, and migrates annually to feed and breed. Winter and spring are spent on the whales' nursery grounds, such as the Valdés Peninsula. Summer and fall are spent on their feeding grounds, where they feast on immense swarms of copepods and other shrimp-like creatures. The location of the southern right whale's ocean pastures is unknown.

Before they were decimated, southern right whales appeared seasonally along the coasts of South America, from Brazil in the east to Peru in the west. Clustered populations inhabited the waters off Australia and New Zealand; around sub-Antarctic islands such as South Georgia and the Kerguelen Islands, and around the southern coast of Africa. In recent years Patagonian whales have been sighted thousands of miles away, near the islands of Tristan da Cunha and South Georgia.

The right whale was the first species of whale to be commercially hunted, evidently since the twelfth century, in the Bay of Biscay. By the sixteenth century it was being pursued as far away as Newfoundland's Grand Banks. Soon northern stocks declined, and whalers increasingly turned to the southern hemisphere for their pursuits. Southern right whales have been hunted since the late seventeenth century, mostly around South Africa and Tasmania, but also off the coasts of Patagonia and Brazil.

In 1780 a single whaling ship killed fifty right whales in the New Gulf. As the great Argentine explorer Francisco Moreno recounted:

Near Chubut lies Bahía Nueva, once the shelter of innumerable whales who livened up the desolate regions with their play. One day, however, whaler fleets discovered this refuge and, according to eye-witnesses, the bay's calm waters shuddered as these mighty and harmless animals struggled, wounded by harpoons. The sea was covered with blood and oil. Within a few days the ferocious instinct of the

beast, which can sometimes remind man of his origins, transformed the site into a horrible slaughterhouse. The thirst for blood and lucre filled the coast with colossal skeletons that are still whitening there. Now silence reigns where everything once was joy.

Before large-scale exploitation began in the early nineteenth century, there are estimated to have been 70,000 southern right whales, most of which were quickly hunted to produce lucrative barrels of oil. By 1850, an estimated 200,000 right whales had been killed worldwide, and the species was considered commercially extinct. Once abundant in every ocean, the right whale is now the rarest of all large whales.

Only in 1935 did the International Whaling Commission finally declare the right whale a protected species, although enforcement was lax. Russian whalers hunted right whales in both hemispheres through the 1960s; 1,200 southern right whales were killed between 1961 and 1962 alone. Several of the Valdés whales still bear severe harpoon scars, possibly from encounters with Russian whalers. Right whales were captured in Brazil until 1973. Chile only gave up the hunt for right whales in the early 1980s, half a century after the species was granted international protection. By the time of the 1986 international whaling moratorium, the world's total right whale population was estimated at just 4,000, less than six percent of its original size.

Today, right whales are virtually extinct in the eastern North Pacific. In the North Atlantic, only about 300 animals remain, inhabiting the waters between their feeding grounds around the Bay of Fundy, Nova Scotia, and their calving grounds off Florida. In this much-traveled ocean, almost sixty percent of right whales bear scars, some with fatal results, from propeller cuts and collisions with ships.

Pollution and entanglement in fishing gear are common hazards for these whales. With so few individuals spread out over vast tracts of ocean, the northern right whale population may never recover: it is the species closest to extinction.

The situation is less grim for the southern right whale. By 1920, there were barely 300 right whales in the entire southern hemisphere, but as they remained far from civilization, they fared better than their northern cousins. Today, over 7,500 right whales roam the southern oceans, two-thirds of which are believed to inhabit the South Atlantic. All of the southern populations appear to be growing at a healthy pace of seven to eight percent per year, and if this trend continues, the number of southern whales should double during the next decade. In the South Pacific, around Australia and New Zealand, right whales appear to be returning to their original haunts, but in the Chilean waters where they were once abundant, there is no population to speak of. Only two sizeable breeding populations remain: the right whales off Patagonia, and a slightly larger group off the coast of South Africa.

In 1975 the government of the Argentine province of Chubut set aside the Gulf of San José as a permanent sanctuary. Whale watching has since been restricted to New Gulf, the larger, southern bay. But in 1979 the law was modified to allow the farming of mollusks, which are grown on ropes that could fatally entangle the whales. For many years they were also disturbed by military exercises that regularly took place in the middle of the gulf until they were suspended in 1984. Despite these disturbances, the whales seem to have fared well. But recent plans to drill for oil in the Gulf of San Jorge, south of the peninsula, may now affect the whales migrating along the coast to their calving grounds at Valdés.

Personalities

The Gulf of San José sparkled in the morning light. All across the water we could see little puffy white clouds—the characteristic V-shaped spout of an exhaling right whale slowly dissipating in the breeze. Right whales can be very playful and active, especially on rough, windy days, but on calm mornings like this one, the whales prefer to rest and sleep. As they lolled about, their dark finless backs resembled logs floating among the

swells. There were several mothers with calves close to shore. Whale mothers and their offspring spend most of their time in shallow waters, where they are protected from marauding orcas and rampant males. Although the whales keep a respectful distance from each other, the giant nursery moves in congruity along the steep limestone cliffs, forming a long chain of animals all the way down the coast. I could hear them breathing in long, rhythmic blows—long, deep "puuuuhs" for the mothers, followed by quick, short "puuhs" from the calves. Some whales were literally snoring, residual water gurgling away in their blowholes. We approached one of the sleepers, but when it heard our boat's motor, it stirred and quickly swam away.

Right whales have real personalities. Some are shy, even terrified, of approaching divers or boats; others are playful and curious. Few are aggressive, although I have seen a young whale slap its tail hard against a boat. Some are outright bold. One whale had the habit of lifting smaller boats gently up on its back. Others are completely uninterested. The ideal whales to dive among are the medium-sized adolescent whales, called subadults. They are curious and love to investigate divers and boats.

That day, a mother and calf were swimming slowly nearby. We throttled the motor some 260 feet (80 m) away from them and waited, since the local whale-watching rules forbid one to position the boat between two whales, to cut across their path, or to approach the boat closer than 150 feet (50 m) to the animals. It is up to the whale whether or not to seek out human company.

The calf was curious. It immediately rushed over to investigate the peculiar new "whale," but its mother interposed herself between it and the boat. The calf swam around her and tried again, but this time she blocked its escape with her tail. Cupping the little calf in her enormous tail she dragged the reluctant youngster away from us with tremendous force. This type of

behavior was not unusual, since most whale mothers are protective of their young.

After a while the pair slowed down and began to float in place. The mother rolled forward, and as her body slowly sank under the water she raised her huge tail high into the air. Gradually her tail flopped over limply, until a tip touched the surface. The calf circled her, slapping the water with its flipper, but to no avail, for the mother was fast asleep. The calf was in a rambunctious mood. With a few strokes of its little tail, it sped over to us and dove under the boat. There it zigzagged back and forth, swimming on its side to get a better look at us. With a hoarse, scratchy "pfff," which sounded as if it was out of breath, the calf appeared at the stern. It was so close that its little calloused head was almost touching the hull. Juan, our skipper and guide, slipped into the water in order to keep the calf interested until I could join him to take my pictures. But unfortunately, when it saw Juan, the calf dove away, leaving only a swirling footprint of water. A few seconds later it resurfaced some fifty feet (15 m) behind Juan, and he paddled toward it. But when he got there, it was gone. "Where is the calf?" Juan shouted, for we had a better view in the boat. No sooner did I point to the footprint right behind him, when the calf suddenly broke the surface vertically beneath him, lifting Juan out of the water with its head, until he rolled down the whale's back and splashed into the sea. Judging this was not the "right" whale to swim with, Juan was back on the boat in a second, fully aware of the dangers of being the plaything of a boisterous puppy the size of an elephant. Though their intentions are good, young whales have yet to learn how to measure their strength and maneuver their bulky bodies.

We continued along the coast, hoping to find a friendly subadult in the shallows. We passed the white cabana of Campamento 39, which is the Wildlife

RIGHT WHALE CALVES ARE RAMBUNCTIOUS, LIKE GIANT PUPPIES. THEY SLAP THEIR FLIPPERS AND TAILS AND SOON LEARN HOW TO BREACH. AS IF TESTING THEIR MOTHER'S PATIENCE, THEY RAM AND SLAP THEM, AND HAVE EVEN BEEN SEEN BREACHING ONTO THEIR MOTHER'S BACKS.

Conservation Society's field camp and base of the longest ongoing study of right whales in the world. Three whales were right in front of the house—roughly thirty feet (10 m) from shore—waving their flippers in the air and rolling from side to side. But the water was so shallow they had stirred up a sandstorm, making photography impossible.

A few miles farther north, at Punta Conos, we found a lone charcoal-colored whale. Before long, Juan and I were in the water, with a plan to descend to the sea floor and wait for the whale to come to us. Slowly we fell through the water until we reached the sandy bottom some fifty feet (15 m) below. Visibility in these latitudes is never very good, and the sea was a milky turquoise color. We could only see about six feet (2 m) in front of us. Unsettled by this, I looked at Juan, and he signaled to wait.

I looked toward the surface, watching the bright light filtering through the wall of water. All was still but for the rhythmic gurgles of our respirators. Suddenly there was darkness: a huge black cloud moved in and was blocking out the sun. But then the cloud moved, light flickered through, and it was suddenly all bright again. A whale had passed right over us! We waited, but unfortunately it never returned. As we were running low on air, we swam back to the boat. Although I hadn't realized it at the time, that was my first underwater encounter with a right whale.

RIGHT WHALES MAY BREACH FOR THE PURE JOY OF IT, AS A SOCIAL DISPLAY, AS A SHOW OF STRENGTH TO CHALLENGE OTHER WHALES, OR AS A FORM OF PLAY AMONG MOTHERS AND CALVES.

Mothers and Calves

At the Valdés Peninsula, the right whale's only true predator is the orca. While a right whale calf has no defense, a single blow with the massive flippers or fluke of its mother could easily crush the much smaller predator's bones. In the presence of orcas, females sometimes swim into a star-like formation—their heads toward their calves in the center, and tails toward the outside—and thrash their massive flukes. Observations of attacks are rare, although occasionally one can find a calf with marks that look like orca bites or an adult with the telltale scar of an attack on the tip of its fluke.

Unfortunately, compared to other large whales, right whales are slow breeders. On average, a female gives birth to a single calf only once every three years. Most right whales reach sexual maturity around seven to eleven years. While it would seem logical for right whale mothers to bear their calves in the tranquil waters of the New Gulf or the Gulf of San José, nobody has ever witnessed a birth. Local fishermen have, however, seen tiny calves with floppy tails and fold marks from being bundled up in the womb. One man, who has fished the Gulf of San José for twenty years, claims to have seen a minute calf and its mother floating among the remnants of what looked like an immense afterbirth. Whale expert Roger Payne has seen females without calves appear later in the season with a calf by their side.

At first, the calf does not part from its mother. When it is about three weeks old it tentatively begins to venture away from her, though it quickly huddles back. Gradually, the calf becomes more adventurous, but when it strays too far, its mother will call it back by vocalizing underwater or by slapping her flipper against the surface. If the calf does not return she may swim over to retrieve it. The calf spends much time circling its mother and experimenting with new activities. It will roll onto its side and back, slap its flippers and tail against the water, and even bang against the mother. This can last for hours, though the mothers usually endure their babies' antics with admirable patience.

Baby Games

Once I watched a calf incessantly butt and ram its resting mother. Eventually she rolled over and it disappeared underneath her to nurse. But the calf remained restless. While its mother hovered peacefully on the surface, the calf repeatedly swam onto her back and blowhole, then slid off again. Lifting one of her enormous flippers, the mother gently patted the hyperactive youngster. Suddenly the calf broke out of the water and leaped right onto her. The mother arched her back and dove under. A few seconds later she surfaced, lifting the little fellow out of the water on her enormous mottled chest. In an unbelievable act of sweetness, she cradled it between her rectangular flippers until it finally appeared to calm down.

By mid-November, at the end of the season, the behavior of mothers and calves abruptly changes. A formidable challenge awaits them. Soon they must leave the tranquil waters of the peninsula's gulfs and travel through the wild southern ocean to their summer feeding grounds, thousands of miles away. Instead of resting and playing, they pace along the peninsula's shores, perhaps to strengthen the calf's muscles for the strenuous voyage ahead. The calf also learns to save energy by swimming beside and slightly behind its mother, whose enormous body displaces so much water it gives the baby a hydrodynamic lift. By the end of the month most mother and calf pairs have left the nursery bays to gather at the mouth of the two gulfs before disappearing into the open ocean.

Most right whale cows remain at the Valdés Peninsula for an average of two and a half months but some stay for almost six. Their days there are marked by courtship; nursing their young; and long, peaceful sleep. They fast throughout the entire sojourn, even during the time they give birth to and suckle their calves. Their energy consumption during this activity is tremendous, requiring the storage of great reserves of blubber; this may explain why female right whales are larger than the males.

Opposite: Newborn calves are about eighteen feet (5.5 m) long, and weigh about three tons. It is likely that they are able to swim within a few hours of birth. To nurse they must dive below their mothers, who squirt massive quantities of creamy milk into their mouths. Every day, the suckling calves grow about an inch (2 to 3 cm) and gain at least 125 pounds (56 kg). By the time they leave the peninsula at almost three months of age they will have grown six to ten feet (2 to 3 m).

Below: The majority of right whale calves are born in July and August. Every year about eighty calves are born, but each season some five to ten calves wash up dead on the peninsula's coast.

SOUTHERN RIGHT WHALE 37

The calf continues to nurse until it returns to the peninsula the following year in the company of its mother. But this time, the mother will stay for only two to eight weeks before heading back out to sea alone. The yearling stays behind, remaining in the peninsula's sheltered bays for three to four months, before migrating to the feeding grounds in late spring.

The mother will nourish herself on the feeding grounds, recovering her depleted fat reserves and strength. She will not mate until the following year. Right whales seem to mate year round, even while on their feeding grounds. Gestation is estimated to last about a year. She will return to give birth at Valdés, two years after she dropped off her previous calf.

Breeding

The first time I visited the Valdés Peninsula was as a tourist with a group of friends from Buenos Aires. One of them had a cousin in Puerto Madryn, and he took us out in his inflatable boat to see the whales. For two weeks we spent every day on the water, eating our lunches in a sheltered bay, always surrounded by whales. I loved listening to their strange blows: as they exhaled, they seemed to be coughing, wheezing, sighing, trumpeting, and even growling. One day, while I was eating a sandwich, I watched an unusual gathering. Whales rumbled and rolled all around. I could not even tell how many there were. All I could see were various whale parts gliding across the surface: a flipper, the corner of a tail, a black and white belly. It was my first introduction to a mating group. Our host, Guillermo, explained that the belly belonged to the female, who was lying upside-down to avoid copulation. Eventually, she would have to turn around to breathe, and that would be when the male lying patiently beneath her, also belly up, would strike. "If he is to get lucky, he must hold his breath for as long as she does, and that might

be up to twenty-five minutes," explained Guillermo. The female was flanked by two other males, who were waiting for her ventral groove to roll past them as she turned around, for right whales mate belly to belly. One of them put a flipper over her. The female swiveled, but remained belly-up. Was he patting her, or trying to push her under?

When the whales breed, some males actually push females underwater so their companions can mate with her as well. They cooperate in such seemingly altruistic mating units, because it affords each individual a better chance to mate. Since females, which can grow up to fifty-six feet (17 m) and weigh over eighty tons, are larger than males, it is difficult for a single male to mate with a defiant female, so they form mating units and spend the season swimming along the coastline trying to entice females from the nursery groups. Some females flee into shallow water to prevent a male from squeezing underneath them; others evade their pursuers by standing on their heads, lifting their tails into the air. But eventually most females are overpowered by a band of males.

Although cooperation is more advantageous than competition, rivalry among the males does exist. When a female becomes accessible, the males struggle to be the first to mate, scratching each other with their callosities.

But the main contest among males takes place at the microscopic level. Because multiple males mate with a single female, they are effectively in sperm competition with each other. The more sperm a male can get into a female, the bigger his chance to father her calf. The most successful is the last, rather than the first, male to mate with her, for he can wash out his competitors' sperm.

With the possible exception of their Arctic cousin,

the bowhead whale, the male right whale has the largest testes in the animal kingdom. While the testes of the 100-foot- (30-m-) long blue whale, the largest animal ever to have lived, weigh only about 150 pounds (70 kg), a right whale's testes can weigh up to a ton, and may be the largest testes ever to have existed on earth. His tapered penis is over six feet (2 m) long, about fourteen percent of his entire body length. It is controllable and movable like an arm, which better enables him to mate with a female that is continually rolling around in the water.

Leviathan Games

The afternoon winds were setting in, stirring up the waters of the gulf. Far in the distance we saw an explo-sion of foam, followed by a thunderous bang. Suddenly, the water erupted just ahead of the boat. A massive whale burst through the surface, shooting into the sky until only the tip of its tail touched the water. Twisting in mid-air it landed on its back, huge white walls of spume shooting up all around it. It breached again, this time right next to our boat, showering us in a cloud of spray. Tons of sea water cascaded in all directions, dis-placed by the whale's gigantic body. The boat rocked vio-lently. The whale in the distance responded by slapping its huge fluke against the water—one, two, three, four— the deafening smacks echoing through the wind. The whale next to us answered by hitting the surface with its giant square flipper. Its friend in the distance slapped the water with its tail.

The most delightful traits of right whales are their curiosity and playfulness. Despite being slow, ponderous swimmers with stocky bodies, right whales are one of the most acrobatic species of whale. Included in their repertoire of antics are spectacular leaps, or breaches; powerful slaps with their flippers and tails; and they have a knack for standing on their heads, waving their tail flukes in the air. On windy days they are considerably more active, probably because they need to make louder sounds to communicate across the rough sea. The whales frolic and drape seaweed over their heads and backs. Dusky dolphins and sea lions are welcome playmates for subadult right whales, who seem to relish and even solicit their company, cavorting with them for hours. The dolphins use the larger whale's pressure wave to ride along next to their bulky heads, while sea lions often spiral around their massive tails.

Right whales also seem to play with any object they can find. When he was studying these animals, Dr. Payne was unable to install tide gauges and stakes because the whales deliberately dislodged and broke them. To the fishermen who harvest mussels in the Gulf of San José, the frisky whales are not only a nuisance, but a real danger. The fishermen dive to depths of about thirty-three to fifty feet (10 to 15 m), deriving their air from long hoses connected to their boats. The curious whales often come to investigate the fishermen, mistaking the swaying anchor lines and air hoses for floating seaweed, waiting to be trailed around. As a result, whenever a whale approaches, the fishermen must interrupt their work and return quickly to the surface. Some even throw stones at the pestering whales, to keep them as far away from the boat as possible, although the stones are no threat to the whales.

A real menace to the whales are the kelp gulls, which descend on them like giant gnats, viciously picking at their skin and blubber. When a whale breaches, the water washes away large flakes of skin, which have always been favorite pickings for scavenging gulls. No longer content with just the old pieces floating around at sea, the birds have acquired a taste for live skin. Landing on a whale's back, they dig deep into the skin with their strong, sharp beaks, gouging out underlying chunks of blubber. The lesions they cause are considerable, laying bare the blubber in white plate-sized craters. Up to twenty such wounds may speckle a whale's back in those areas most exposed to the air when they swim on the surface.

The problem is a very recent one. In the early 1970s there were no whales with visible skin problems, but by the end of the decade, the first gulls were seen gouging out pieces of blubber. This phenomenon all began in an isolated bay in the Gulf of San José, but other gulls have caught on quickly, and such attacks have been rising ever since. Since 1986 attacks have also been reported in the New Gulf. This constant harassment of the whales may be seriously affecting their well-being. Gull harassment increased five-fold between 1984 and 1995, and almost doubled in the next two years. One of the contributing factors may be an explosion of the gull population due to man-made food sources, such as Puerto Madryn's three industrial fish processing plants and the town's open-air garbage dump.

Opposite: SOMETIMES WHALES BREACH TO CHASE AWAY KELP GULLS THAT TRY TO PICK AT THEIR SKIN.

Below: LIKE A WOODPECKER JABBING AT A TREE, A KELP GULL LANDS ON A RIGHT WHALE TO PICK AT AND EAT ITS SKIN AND BLUBBER. REACTING AS IF STUNG BY A BEE, THE WHALE VIOLENTLY ARCHES ITS BACK AND THROWS ITS HEAD UP AS IT TRIES TO RID ITSELF OF THE ATTACKER.

Right: ONE OF THE MOST DISTINGUISHING FEATURES OF RIGHT WHALES ARE THE THICK PATCHES OF ROUGH, CALLOUSED SKIN ADORNING THEIR HEADS. THE WHALES ARE BORN WITH THESE CALLOSITIES, AND EACH INDIVIDUAL WEARS A UNIQUE PATTERN OF SUCH VARIED DESIGNS, THAT IT ALLOWS FOR THE WHALE'S IDENTIFICATION THROUGHOUT ITS LIFE. THE CALLOSITIES ARE MORE DEVELOPED IN MALES, PROBABLY BECAUSE THEY USE THEM AS SCRATCHY WEAPONS TO BATTLE EACH OTHER. MOST CALLOSITIES ARE GRAY, BUT ARE TINGED WHITE, WITH YELLOW, ORANGE, AND PINK HUES, BY THOUSANDS OF PARASITIC CYAMIDS.

Opposite: A CLUSTER OF CYAMIDS, THE CRAB-LIKE WHALE LICE, CLINGS TO A WHALE'S SKIN. RIGHT WHALES ARE HOSTS TO THOUSANDS OF THESE TINY CRUSTACEANS, WHICH SPEND THEIR ENTIRE LIVES ON THEIR HOSTS, FEEDING ON THEIR SKIN. UNABLE TO SWIM, THEY WILL DIE IF THEY FALL OFF A WHALE, AND ARE FOUND ON NO OTHER ANIMALS OR SURFACES. THEY CLING TO THE WHALE'S CALLOSITIES AND BODY GROOVES SUCH AS THEIR EYES, MOUTH, BLOWHOLE, AND GENITAL SLIT.

Two-thirds of the gull attacks are aimed at existing lesions, and gulls have been seen to enlarge old wounds throughout a season. Some scientists are concerned that the birds may be infecting the whale's wounds with microorganisms from the dump. Others believe that the lesions are in fact a form of eczema caused by pollution, and that the gulls, rather than being the culprit, are merely taking advantage of the exposed areas of blubber.

Nursing mothers and their calves are the most vulnerable, for they spend long periods resting at the surface, where the birds peck away furiously. The giant animals immediately arch their backs and sound in agony, but the gulls follow the diving whales from above, and as soon as they resurface, besiege them again. Some desperate whales try to defend themselves using their flippers and flukes. A study by Vicky Rowntree, Dr. Payne's colleague, found that in 1995, females were under siege for almost a quarter of the day, and their calves were also being attacked, with gull assaults interrupting their normal resting and nursing cycles. Compared to undisturbed animals, the besieged whales spend three times as much of their day traveling at fast speeds.

While at Valdés, the fasting females rest to conserve their blubber reserves. Now, instead of using their blubber to fatten their calves for the long journey ahead, they are forced to waste vital energy reserves evading the gulls. It takes up to an hour after an attack for them to resume resting and nursing their calves.

The effects of the kelp gulls on the reproductive success of the right whale could be tragic.

The Whale-Watching Industry

Unfortunately, it is not only the gulls that harass the whales. Tourism has increased dramatically. In 1987, 5,200 people traveled to see the whales; in 1996, six tour operators shuttled 53,000 tourists in 4,200 sorties. The following year they carried 74,000 whale watchers.

Maneuvering around a whale requires caution and experience. Although local regulations are very strict and better enforced than in most other places in the world, two studies conducted between 1993 and 1995 concluded that in 80 percent of their trips, tour boat captains violated protective guidelines. When boats approached to within approximately 150 feet (50 m) of a whale, half the whales took evasive action. At twice that distance, only a third of the whales retreated, and at four times the distance, only 14 percent tried to escape the camera-toting tourists. As with the gull attacks, the targets were mainly mothers and calves. In as many as 39 percent of the voyages, the whales were intercepted, encircled, or chased. Most animals responded by abruptly changing their swimming direction. Vertical slash marks can be seen on the backs of some whales, the result of the boat propellers of renegade captains.

The whales in the San José sanctuary are much calmer than their cousins in the New Gulf, where vessel traffic has risen more than tenfold in the last two decades. Mothers with calves travel at similar speeds in both gulfs, probably because the little calves are unable to swim very fast. But in the New Gulf, subadult and adult whales swim considerably faster and appear more erratic. They have less defined swimming routes, and often abruptly change their course.

Top and middle left: THE RIGHT WHALE'S TWIN BLOWHOLES PRODUCE A BUSHY V-SHAPED SPOUT THAT CAN REACH OVER SIXTEEN FEET (5 M) IN HEIGHT. UNFORTUNATELY, IT WAS THE WHALE'S CONSPICUOUS BLOW THAT GAVE IT AWAY TO THE WHALERS OF YORE.

Bottom left: INSTEAD OF TEETH, THE RIGHT WHALE POSSESSES A LONG BALEEN, A CURTAIN OF ABOUT 240 BRISTLY PLATES ABOUT NINE FEET (2.8 M) IN LENGTH, THAT HANGS FROM ITS UPPER JAWS. THE WHALE FEEDS BY SKIMMING THE SURFACE, STRAINING TONS OF TINY ORGANISMS OUT OF THE WATER USING ITS BALEEN. THE WHALES PRIMARILY FAST THROUGHOUT THEIR FOUR-MONTH SOJOURN AT VALDÉS, ALTHOUGH THERE IS SOME EVIDENCE THAT THEY MAY HAVE AN OCCASIONAL SNACK. SPORADICALLY WHALES ARE SEEN SWIMMING AT THE SURFACE WITH OPEN MOUTHS—WE DO NOT KNOW WHETHER THEY ARE FEEDING OR JUST COOLING OFF.

Opposite: AT THE VALDÉS PENINSULA, MOST WHALE SIGHTINGS OCCUR BETWEEN JUNE AND DECEMBER, BUT SOME WHALES ARRIVE AS EARLY AS APRIL, WHILE OTHERS LEAVE AS LATE AS JANUARY. IN RECENT YEARS SOLITARY ANIMALS HAVE BEEN SEEN YEAR-ROUND.

All factors combined, the right whales today face considerable hazards. Can they endure increasing numbers of tourists? Could persistent harassment by boats and gulls eventually drive them away from their ancestral breeding grounds and affect their reproductive success? Are they resilient enough to accommo- date such changes in their environment? The answers to these questions do not seem hopeful. Just when these vulnerable creatures made an almost miraculous recovery from near extinction, their future has become once again as precarious as ever.

Underwater Encounters

The sun was shining in a blue, cloudless sky, reflecting in the giant mirror of the sea. Out in the deep waters of the New Gulf, far away from any bottom sediments and runoffs from land, the sea was the most intense jade-green color I had ever seen. A grayish whale and a black whale of similar size were cautiously circling our boat. After a while the black whale came alongside. There it hovered like a huge round airship in liquid space, rising up and down in place by controlling the air in its lungs. As it exhaled a sweet-smelling cloud of mist swept over us, forming sticky droplets that fogged my camera lens.

I slid down the side of the boat as silently as possible. The whales were nowhere to be seen. The rays of the midday sun filtered down like the tentacles of a Portuguese man-of-war. The bottomless emptiness stretching before me was terrifying. Clinging to the boat's ladder, I took a few deep breaths before letting go—which was like cutting an umbilical cord.

The skipper signaled me to swim straight ahead. I swam slowly, deliberately. The boat grew smaller and smaller, but he still waved and pointed. Suddenly I saw an enormous shadow, moving ever so slowly, beneath me. My heart began beating so fast I thought I might pass out. I glanced around me in utter panic. But the shadow disappeared.

Then I saw what at first was just a movement from the corner of my eye, until I made out the gleaming white callosities of a right whale. Rising up diagonally through the thick, foggy layers of green was a huge black whale, coming straight at me. Although the whale swam toward me very slowly, the draft of its enormous body created such a suction of water that I was swept toward it until I hovered just inches above its broad black back. I dared not move, afraid I would bump into it and suffer the same fate as one diver I had seen in a video, who touched a right whale, causing it to bolt off in terror, nearly knocking the diver over.

Slowly the whale glided away, still only inches beneath me. Its enormous tail almost brushed against my legs, but the whale appeared to know exactly where we were in relation to each other, and swam past with unbelievable precision and care. As it faded away into the murky green, a strange intuition told me to turn around, and there I saw the second whale. Floating six feet (2 m) under the surface, it was looking me up and down with its big cow-like eye.

Suddenly fearless, I dove down toward the whale. Its eyes followed my every move. I was so close I could make out clusters of whale lice in the grooves of its lids. It blinked, but never once flinched or tried to swim away. The two whales circled me, coming and going. But when they both faded away into the turbid green my fears returned, and I paddled back to the boat as fast as I could.

Just as I was climbing onto the deck I felt something brush against me, and realized that the whales had followed me back to the boat. One of them lifted its tail out of the water and gently flopped it over me. I did not move. Swimming by ever so slowly, it brushed its rubbery tail all over my body, face, and head with unbelievable gentleness. I had just been caressed by a whale!

SMACKING THEIR TAILS AGAINST THE SURFACE MAY BE A FORM OF COMMUNICATION, ESPECIALLY WHEN THE NOISE FROM ROUGH SEAS DROWNS A WHALE'S NATURAL VOICE. WHEN A WHALE STARTS TO TAILLOB OR BREACH, IT IS OFTEN ANSWERED BY ANOTHER WHALE TAILLOBBING OR BREACHING SOMEWHERE IN THE DISTANCE—ON VERY WINDY DAYS, THE ENTIRE GULF CAN BE FULL OF TAILLOBBING AND BREACHING WHALES. BUT ON CALM DAYS, ESPECIALLY AFTER STORMY WEATHER, THE WHALES APPEAR TO BE IN DEEP SLEEP.

Southern Elephant Seal (Mirounga leonina)

THE SOUTHERN ELEPHANT SEAL, THE
LARGEST SEAL IN THE WORLD, IS FOUND
THROUGHOUT THE SOUTHERN OCEAN SUR-
ROUNDING THE ANTARCTIC CONTINENT.
UNLIKE OTHER SEALS OF THE REGION, IT
RARELY VENTURES INTO THE PACK ICE.

A New Season Begins

Winters at the Valdés Peninsula are solitary and bleak.
Rarely do the skies clear to allow a feeble, distant light to
filter through. An oppressive cloud blanket hangs low
across the horizon and rain drizzles for days on end,
until a sudden torrential shower explodes over the land.
The cold, unabating wind howls across the wide-open
spaces, rattling over lifeless gray bushes and plunging
down steep cliffs to the vast empty coastline. Swirling
curtains of mist and wet sand sweep the barren shores,
pouring over the rocks and squeezing into every nook
and cranny, as if in desperate pursuit of a sign of life.

It has now been almost three months since the last
penguin, seal, or whale swam along these coasts, and the
cold, dark days in this desolate landscape bear heavily
on the soul. Nearly a week has gone by since I last
stepped out to collect some firewood from the tin-roofed
barn. Holed up in the warmth of the small ranger station, a fire crackling away in the grate, I shuddered at
the thought of going out. Yet, a few minutes later, I was
standing outside, packed up like an arctic explorer, with
ski goggles, heavy boots, and thick gloves.

I followed the narrow trail that led down to the
beach, my eyes scanning the horizon. It was late August,
and the austral winter was nearing its end. It seemed
unimaginable that in just a few more weeks this place
would be transformed into a cradle of life and these
empty beaches would be teeming with crawling, yapping, bellowing seals.

It was high tide, and I walked briskly along the
shoreline, trying to avoid the ripples that washed up to
my feet. I looked up and suddenly realized that I was
standing just three feet away from an enormous gray
blob: a bull elephant seal. He was lying on his side,
exposing his broad, oversized belly and calloused chest,
the proud scar of a seasoned warrior. Two peg-like
canines protruded like vampire teeth from the side of his
mouth, framing his thick, elephantine nose. He rose
from his death-like slumber. "Pfff!" A salty snort broke
the silence. In less than a second, he inhaled and
exhaled, causing his nostrils to flare and shut tightly like
two waterproof valves. These air-breathing mammals
are so in tune with their marine environment that an
innate reflex causes them to hold their breath for inter-

vals of ten minutes or more, even while they sleep on land. I have witnessed them snoozing around tidal pools with their heads in the water and their bodies on land, as if it made no difference at all.

The Valdés Peninsula is one of the elephant seal's northernmost breeding colonies. Spring comes early to this region, and the annual breeding cycle begins here almost three weeks before it does in any of the circumpolar rookeries. The huge bull in front of me was one of the first arrivals of the new season.

This beach near Punta Hercules is one of the traditional breeding areas, drawing some of the biggest males and largest harems. Being one of the first to arrive in such a coveted spot has drastically increased this bull's chances of obtaining and keeping his own harem of females. The instinct that brought him here will soon lure his competitors, and by the second week of September, most alpha (breeding) bulls will have established their supremacy over a collection of cows. Those that come too late are condemned to prowl from harem to harem looking for a chance to displace an established beachmaster in a bloody battle. In the worst case, they will not have a chance to breed this year.

The southern elephant seal (*Mirounga leonina*) is the larger of two species of elephant seal, whose habitat is

Left and opposite: DURING THEIR TERRESTRIAL PHASE, ELEPHANT SEALS FAST AND SPEND MOST OF THEIR TIME SLEEPING TO CONSERVE VITAL ENERGY RESERVES. MOTIONLESS GIANTS, THEY RESEMBLE WET OVAL ROCKS STREWN ALONG THE BEACH AND BLEND PERFECTLY INTO THE LANDSCAPE. ELEPHANT SEALS ARE ENDOWED WITH A GENEROUS COAT OF GREASY BLUBBER, WHICH IN LARGE ANIMALS MAY BE UP TO SIX INCHES (15 CM) THICK. THE WRAPPING OF FAT INSULATES THEM FROM THE COLD ANTARCTIC CURRENTS, BUT IS ALSO A LARDER FOR LEAN TIMES, AND PROVIDES VITAL ENERGY FOR THE LONG FASTS DURING THE MOLTING AND BREEDING SEASONS. THE FATTEST AND BIGGEST BULLS CAN SURVIVE THE LONGEST TENURE ON THE BEACHES, AN ESSENTIAL FACTOR FOR MATING WITH AS MANY FEMALES AS POSSIBLE. SOME BULLS MAY SHED AS MUCH AS FORTY PERCENT OF THEIR BODY WEIGHT DOMINATING THEIR WIVES AND BATTLING OTHER MALES.

separated by opposing hemispheres. Its close cousin, the northern elephant seal (*Mirounga angustirostris*) inhabits the northeastern Pacific, from California to Alaska. Elephant seals belong to the family of true seals (*Phocidae*) and are distinct from sea lions, which belong to the family of "eared seals" (*Otariidae*), which have a diminutive ear flap, not found on true seals. Elephant seals can dive deeper and stay down longer than sea lions, although they have less agility on land, since their hind limbs are fused and point backward, forcing them to crawl along on their bellies like gigantic caterpillars. Elephant seals use their lumbar muscles to propel themselves through the water with their hindflippers; sea lions use their foreflippers to swim.

With the exception of sperm whales, elephant seals can dive deeper and for longer than any other marine mammal. Southern elephant seals are the largest of all seals, and the sexual dimorphism, or disparity in size between males and females, exceeds that of any other mammal. Adult males are about sixteen feet (5 m) long and can weigh over three tons, four times more than the nine-foot (3-m) long females, which can weigh as much as 1,800 pounds (800 kg). Elephant seal sultans proudly rule over the largest harems of females in the entire seal community. With multiple doughy chins and soft, plump bodies, the voluptuous cows are irresistible to the frantic bulls, and competition for them is fierce.

Domination

Following puberty, the male elephant seal develops an inflatable snout that hangs in front of its face like an elephant's trunk. A bull's trunk, a sign of sexual maturity, reaches its full splendor when he is about ten years old. Dominance hierarchies tend to be structured by age, size, and previous experience, all of which are

symbolized by a well-developed organ, a mere glance at which may send a younger bull packing.

Only the true "big noses" are allowed to mate, and most males are relegated to the unfortunate role of frustrated onlookers. Until their noses begin to grow with puberty in their sixth year, the young males are barely distinguishable from the females. They play-fight among themselves, mimicking the fights of adult bulls. By the time they are seven, they sport noticeable noses and the dermal shield on their chest has grown thicker from their sparring; however, they are still too small to confront a seasoned bull. It is safer for them to practice for the brutal battles of future years by challenging other subadults of similar size. They tend to stay clear from the main breeding congregations, dodging the prying eyes of the sultans. Only the occasional solitary female will succumb to these fiery young males, but these are few and far between.

Below: THE LONG CLAWS ON A BULL'S MASSIVE FLIPPER REMIND US OF THEIR DISTANT ANCESTRY AS TERRESTRIAL ANIMALS.

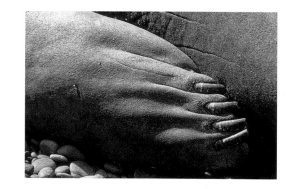

The next season they return with sizeable snouts. Their chests are scratched and creased from the previous year's juvenile battles. Now in their eighth year, they have lengthened by some three feet (1 m) since their noses first began to grow. With their testosterone levels running high, they are aggressive and ready for a challenge. Those who arrive early may become the lucky first-time rulers of minor harems, but most will linger jealously on the periphery of established ones. There, in the outer reaches of the sultan's realm, while his attention is directed elsewhere, they furtively mate with some of his wives.

A successful beachmaster is never off duty. Unless he continuously proves his superiority he is quickly relieved of his position. The first step is to alert other bulls of his presence. From time to time, he produces a gargling belch of impressive volume that resonates through his inflatable nose; it is echoed by other males along the beach. He is surrounded by enemies—zealous contenders for the harem's Rubensesque beauties—who ceaselessly prowl the shallows searching for a good spot for an ambush. But most of their attacks are half-hearted attempts. To gate-crash a beachmaster's territory is risky, and most contests end before they start. Male elephant seals always size each other up first, and once a

A Battle of Goliaths

*I*t was a breezy day in early October. The colossal beachmaster at the center of the colony was going about the daily business of tending his wives. He shoveled over to a pale, chamois-colored cow and her fluffy, black pup. In his frenzy he rolled right over the bleating youngster. Then he heaved himself on top of the cow, pinning her down with the crushing weight of his enormous body. Only her whiskered face was visible under his huge frame, and her dark eyes bulged. He then rolled next to her, grabbing her with his flipper, his long nails digging into her hide. She struggled to free herself of the forceful embrace, but he bit her neck until his peg-like teeth buried deep into her flesh, causing her to bellow in distress. Gradually she gave up the struggle and he mated with her, side by side.

Suddenly something caught his attention and he disengaged. From the other side of the beach sounded a loud, rattling roar from ferocious-looking competition. The beachmaster opened his mouth in a wide yawn and released a shockingly rude sequence of belches. Steam

rose from his pink gums into the cold Patagonian air as from the mouth of some mythological dragon. The other bull roared back and began to encroach on the harem. The beachmaster rose angrily into the air, but the trespasser remained undeterred. With full power, he charged into the colony.

The beachmaster was facing his match in size and strength: the alpha male from the adjacent harem. For one week now the intruder had been herding his harem of females toward his counterpart's territory. Now that both breeding groups were rubbing shoulders, he had come to conquer the rest.

Suddenly the beachmaster raised his upper body high into the air until he stood as tall as a man. This is the most serious of all threatening displays, and it would persuade any smaller bull to flee in absolute panic. The intruder mirrored the threat, lifting his chest and tail into the air and rocking back and forth on his belly like an upturned horseshoe. Then with an enormous bang, he lunged forward, three and a half tons of fat hitting the ground as pebbles flew in all directions. Pushing with his foreflippers, he bulldozed up the beach, his massive body quivering like jelly as layers of blubber reverberated in ripples from head to tail.

The beachmaster raced toward the trespasser with unexpected agility. Within seconds their bodies collided with a loud, dull "thwack." Pressing against each other with their massive chests, they pushed each other along the beach like two sumo wrestlers trying to throw each other off balance. They reared back, then crashed into each other again with full force.

The attacker swiped at the resident bull like a striking snake. His gaping jaws buried deep into the broad shield of thickened skin on his neck. Streams of blood gushed into the sand, but the beachmaster appeared unperturbed. The two opponents again pushed and shoved furiously along the beach, their obese bodies

appearing to swell with rage. Suddenly, the beachmaster broke loose and ripped through his rival's soft nose with one of his sharp pointed teeth, severing it right through the middle.

With crimson flesh flapping in front of his face the invader dashed toward the sea. Thick tractor trails marked the path where he dragged his bulky body from the battle site to the water. He ducked under the waves and disappeared for several seconds, but the raging beachmaster shot after him with terrorizing speed. This battle of goliaths continued on the shallow banks in front of the colony as the bull elephant seals hacked away at each other among explosive clouds of spray. In equal matches like this one, it is endurance that defines a champion. Eventually, the aggressor gave up and dove

away. His strategy had backfired and he had lost everything. But he would be back to fight another year.

Bloodied and exhausted, the victor returned to his prize: a harem of almost twice as many blubbery females as before. It was his physiological duty to impregnate as many of them as possible and propagate his champion genes, and he immediately set about to the task.

younger bull realizes his physical disadvantage, he usually retreats. A mere glance from a seasoned patriarch is sufficient to make a young male back off. Should it not be enough, the patriarch will lift his head and roar a warning.

The Cycles of a Year

An elephant seal's year is divided into four cycles: two on land, and two in the ocean. Truly amphibious, they live at the interface of land and sea. Elephant seals haul out on land for the breeding season, which lasts from late August through early November, and for the molting season from mid-December through March. During their biannual forays at sea, they cover distances ranging from 1,200 to 4,700 miles (2,000 to 7,500 km).

Not all of the 43,000 elephant seals that visit the peninsula return at the same time. Males, females, and newborn pups dominate the beaches in the austral spring. Numbers peak during the first week of October, at the height of the breeding season, when almost 25,000 animals are on the beaches. Juveniles and yearlings, on the other hand, stay away during the breeding season. Their time to visit the peninsula is during the summer months, when they share the area with molting females. Adult bulls come ashore to molt in the early days of autumn.

Elephant seals follow their biological clocks with astonishing precision. The breeding season begins in the last two weeks of August, when the first gigantic bulls haul out onto the shores to reserve the best spots along the coast. The first females reach the peninsula about a week later, but most arrive in September. Almost all are in the advanced stages of pregnancy. Laden with their unborn young, with enormous effort they drag their swollen bodies up the beach, where

they are immediately incorporated into the dominion of a bull. Within less than a week after arriving, they give birth to a single coal-black pup. Most pups are born within the week spanning the last days of September and first days of October.

The female suckles her pups for approximately three weeks. In the last few days before weaning her pup, the cow becomes sexually receptive and is bred by the local beachmaster. Sexual activity peaks between the second and third week of October. A couple days after mating, she abruptly abandons her pup as hunger draws her back to the sea.

Nursing takes a severe toll on the cows. Some will shed up to 770 pounds (350 kg) while captive to their greedy offspring. Emaciated and dangerously low on fat reserves, they must replenish their critical blubber mass. By the end of the month most females have left the rookeries for their feeding grounds off Argentina's broad continental shelf. For two months they gorge themselves with food before returning to land to molt. By some ingenious invention of nature the newly pregnant females are allowed their much-needed rest and time to regain lost energy reserves: the fertilized egg does not implant itself in the womb for another four months. The process of delayed implantation also allows the seals to breed at fixed annual intervals,

timing the birth of their pups with the most favorable season of the year.

After their mothers have left, the pups try to steal milk and affection from other cows, but are soon chased away from the main rookery. There, at the edges of the breeding colony, they encounter fellow weaners and last year's brood, which have come to molt. As the weaners and yearlings huddle together for warmth and company, they are practically indistinguishable from each other. After a year of having to fend for themselves, many yearlings are considerably thinner than the well-nourished weaners. The weaner pups remain on the beach for another four to six weeks, until sometime in November or early December, when instinct and hunger drive them to their real home, the sea. Their excess body fat provides enough nourishment for a while, though they will continue to lose weight during the first year. If they survive the first season at sea, they will return to the peninsula the following year to join a fellow class of skinny yearlings.

After the departure of the harem, the breeding bulls stay behind to assure themselves that none of the females have skipped their notice. By the time they leave in mid-November, they have spent about ten weeks on land, fasting and fighting. In an effort to keep all of their wives in check and intruders at bay, they have lost up to 40 percent of their original body mass. Mere shadows of September's enormous champions, they, too, must now return to the sea to feed.

During the month of November, two-thirds of the animals strewn about along the pebbled shoreline are yearlings and juveniles which have come to land for the forty-day molt until mid-December. During this time, their old coat gradually peels off and is replaced with a new crop of silvery fur. Most of the females return to molt in the last days of the year. By mid-January, practically all the elephant seals basking under the summer sky are molting females. They will leave in the early days of February, about the time when the first adult males haul out for their annual molt. It is the colossal bulls that will occupy the coasts throughout the month of March. With lustrous new coats, the seals enter the longest cycle of the year: an eight-month period during which they will not see or touch land, as they hunt in the deep waters beyond the continental shelf.

Champions of the Deep

Elephant seals prey mainly on deep-water squid, and all feeding occurs during diving. They will dive virtually continuously during their entire time at sea, needing little more than two to three minutes rest at the surface. One particular female elephant seal off the Valdés Peninsula dove 3,587 times in fifty-eight days, never spending more than five minutes at the surface.

Physiologically, an elephant seal's capacity to dive verges on the miraculous, and only sperm whales are known to dive to such depths. Most dives extend 1,000 to 2,000 feet (300 to 600 m) and last about twenty minutes, but one Valdés elephant seal bull was observed to dive to a staggering 5,000 feet (1,560 m), the deepest dive ever recorded for a seal. Off Macquarie Island, a southern elephant seal female broke the record for the longest time underwater by an air-breathing vertebrate, staying down for an incredible two hours. Only a handful of elephant seals have been fitted out with time-depth recorders, which biologists glue onto their heads. Considering such amazing results with a limited number of animals, it is likely that these super-divers may be able to venture to yet greater depths for even longer periods of time.

How do these air-breathing, warm-blooded

THE DIFFERENCE IN SIZE BETWEEN MALE AND FEMALE ELEPHANT SEALS IS MORE PRONOUNCED THAN IN ANY OTHER MAMMAL IN THE WORLD. ADULT MALES CAN GROW TO OVER SIXTEEN FEET (5 M) AND CAN WEIGH ALMOST FOUR TONS. IT IS NOT INCONCEIVABLE THAT AN ADULT MALE OF OVER 6,500 POUNDS (3,000 KG) COULD MATE WITH A THREE-YEAR-OLD FEMALE WEIGHING ONLY ONE-TENTH AS MUCH. ON AVERAGE, THE MALE IS ABOUT THREE TO FOUR TIMES HEAVIER THAN THE FEMALE. ADULT FEMALES ARE ABOUT NINE FEET (3 M) LONG AND WEIGH AROUND 1,300 POUNDS (600 KG).

Giving Birth

When I lived at Caleta Valdés, one of the main elephant seal rookeries was right at my doorstep. But though I waited daily from dawn to dusk, I had not witnessed a birth, although every morning, when I went down to the beach, I saw at least one tiny newborn pup. After almost two weeks, I had learned the hard way that most births occur under the safe blanket of night.

My chances for seeing a birth were dwindling. It was mid-October and most pups were well on their way to being weaned. There were only two pregnant cows left, one on each side of the widespread colony. Unable to see both of them at the same time, I was forced to run from one to the other, with the fear that I would always be at the wrong place at the wrong time. Eventually I decided to focus on the smaller of the two. She was probably a first-time mother, which would give both of us a little more time. I hoped it would be only a matter of hours before she succumbed to the swelling urge inside of her.

I sat on a little ledge above the beach and watched her every move. She shuffled about in a futile effort to get more comfortable, digging her snout into the sand and flippering some of it onto her back. She lay there, barrel-bellied and helpless. Soon the evening sun would disappear behind the tall cliffs, ending yet another unsuccessful wait.

But she began to move, dragging her swollen body over the pebbles. Every couple of feet she paused, her belly rising and falling in quick, strained breaths. Suddenly, she arched her back, lifting her head and tail, until her body formed a perfect, tall U-shape. Elephant seals are incredibly flexible, and can touch their tails with their heads. While bending backward she glanced at me with the big black eyes of an oriental doll, staring straight into my soul. Streams of thick, glassy tears ran down her cheeks. Although this is actually the mucous protection that defends a seal's eyes against salt water, it was as though she was crying in agony.

The female's hind flippers then spread apart like two big fans, cradling a dark orange balloon that appeared and disappeared from inside her. Again and again she lifted her body high off the ground as if trying to defy gravity. Suddenly the balloon burst and the smudged face of a pup emerged from between her flippers, bleating weakly. With the pup still inside her, the mother shuffled desperately along the beach, dragging the pup along between her flippers, his tiny head bouncing dangerously over the pebbles. Struggling to free herself of the pup, she twisted and turned until the amniotic sac and fluid emerged with a splash.

In this arid landscape nothing goes to waste, and a flock of gulls and petrels greedily awaited the afterbirth. One particularly coy bird tried to pick at the pup's umbilical cord, but the mother pushed it away with a quick flick of her strong tail. The pup struggled to free itself from the gauzy membrane. His mother did not help it, nor lick it clean, nor sever the umbilical cord, which would eventually fall off by itself. Those are the instincts of terrestrial mammals.

The pup yapped in a high-pitched tone, and its mother responded in low, deep "baahs." She slowly leaned toward it and gently nuzzled its tiny, wet snout. They began to bond, imprinting on each other's voices and scent. Not quite knowing what to look for, the pup explored her warm, blood-encrusted belly. It would be a couple of hours before it would begin to nurse.

Opposite: NURSING FEMALES CAN LOSE UP TO SOME 800 POUNDS (350 KG) SUCKLING THEIR PUPS. PUPS BORN TO LARGER MOTHERS ARE SUBSTANTIALLY HEAVIER AT WEANING THAN THEIR LESS FORTUNATE SIBLINGS. FATTER MOTHERS SIMPLY HAVE MORE TO GIVE, PROVIDING THEIR PUPS WITH A HEAD START TOWARD ADULTHOOD.

Below: AT THE MOMENT OF BIRTH, AN ELEPHANT SEAL PUP TAKES ITS FIRST BREATH OF AIR.

mammals manage to stretch a couple of breaths of air such a long way? How can they survive on such low levels of oxygen? And how can they withstand the crushing pressure of thousands of tons of sea water without suffering decompression sickness? As a seal begins to dive it exhales, taking only a small amount of air down with it, which reduces the chance of nitrogen build-up. The increasing pressure collapses its flexible ribs and lungs, and the tissues inside its middle-ear sinus swell, filling noxious air spaces. This forces the remaining air into areas of the body where it can not be absorbed by the blood and which are less susceptible to pressure.

Female elephant seals, which may spend as much as nine months a year at sea, descend so deep that the crushing pressure is deemed to collapse their lungs for up to 95 percent of their dives. Since they dive almost continuously, their lungs are collapsed during most of their time at sea.

Some scientists believe that an elephant seal might be sleeping during its descent: as it plunges deeper into the icy darkness, the seal gradually shuts off certain parts of its body. Its body temperature and metabolic rate decrease, and its heartbeat slows, enabling it to use lower levels of oxygen. Its pulse falls by half, limiting the blood flow to the muscles and internal organs. Deeper yet, its pulse may slow down to as little as two or three beats per minute, redirecting blood to the brain. In one recorded case the time between heart beats reached twenty-six seconds. Once all oxygen reserves have been used up the seal can continue to dive for a while by burning sugars until the build-up of dangerous acid wastes finally forces it to surface.

The Valdés Colony

The southern elephant seal colony at the Valdés Peninsula is unusual. Elephants seals generally breed on sub-Antarctic islands, making the peninsula their only continental breeding ground. With the exception of a small rookery on Gough Island, it is also their northernmost large breeding colony. But most interesting of all, the Valdés Peninsula stands alone as the world's only southern elephant seal rookery that is growing. The colony has expanded markedly over the last two decades, and is presently increasing at a steady rate of 3.5 percent per year. For unknown reasons, the numbers of southern elephant seals have been falling dramatically over the past decades. With the one exception—the island of South Georgia,

Left: DURING THE ANNUAL MOLTING SEASON THE ELEPHANT SEALS COME TO LAND TO EXCHANGE THEIR SHABBY OLD COATS FOR NEW SKINS. PEELING BACK FROM THE BELLY OUTWARD, THEIR DULL, RUSTY-HUED HIDE FALLS OFF IN PATCHES, REVEALING A SHINING CHARCOAL UNDERCOAT. ALTHOUGH THE SEALS RUB ASSIDUOUSLY AGAINST EACH OTHER AND AGAINST ROCKS AND PEBBLES TO LOOSEN THEIR SKIN, THIS PROCESS MAY TAKE FORTY DAYS OR MORE. SINCE THE GROWTH-PROMOTING BLOOD SUPPLY TO THEIR SKIN IS GREATLY INCREASED AT THIS TIME, THEY ARE PRONE TO HEAT LOSS AND SENSITIVE TO COLD SEA WATER, AND CAN NOT RETURN TO FEED AT SEA UNTIL THE LAST DREARY PATCH HAS BEEN SHED.

Opposite: ELEPHANT SEALS HAVE RECORD-BREAKING AQUATIC ENDURANCE. COMPARED TO TERRESTRIAL MAMMALS, SEALS HAVE ALMOST TWICE AS MUCH BLOOD IN RELATION TO BODY SIZE, HIGHER LEVELS OF HEMOGLOBIN, AND LARGER RED BLOOD CELLS, ALLOWING THEM TO STORE MORE OXYGEN. THEY ALSO HAVE EXCEPTIONALLY HIGH LEVELS OF MYOGLOBIN, WHICH ALLOWS THE STORAGE OF OXYGEN IN THEIR MUSCLES. THESE PHYSIOLOGICAL ADAPTATIONS ARE COMMON AMONG MARINE MAMMALS, BUT THEY CONTRIBUTE TO THE ELEPHANTS SEAL'S ABILITY TO DIVE TO UNCHARTED LIMITS, THE MECHANICS OF WHICH SCIENTISTS ONLY PARTLY UNDERSTAND. RIVALED ONLY BY SPERM WHALES, ELEPHANT SEALS CAN DIVE DEEPER THAN 5,000 FEET (1,500 M) AND STAY UNDERWATER FOR AS LONG AS TWO HOURS.

where numbers appear to be stagnant—the South Atlantic rookeries have shrunk at alarming levels of 50 to 90 percent over the past forty years.

The 43,000 elephant seals at the Valdés Peninsula may be only a small fraction of the 750,000 animals roaming the southern oceans, almost half of which breed on the island of South Georgia, but the importance of the Valdés colony is growing steadily. Should the negative trends elsewhere continue, the peninsula could eventually play a significant role in the conservation of the species.

One of the factors influencing the expansion of the peninsula's colony may be the abundance of fishing stocks close to the rookery. The waters surrounding the peninsula are temperate compared to the icy ocean, where elephant seals usually forage. The Valdés elephant seals reach their feeding grounds along the edge of the continental shelf, 300 miles (500 km) east of the rookery, in less than three days. South Georgian and other elephant seals from sub-Antarctic rookeries have to swim markedly farther on an empty stomach, to more southern fishing grounds along the Antarctic shelf, although these waters are exceptionally productive.

ONLY A FEW DAYS OLD, THE PUP (LEFT),
STILL HAS A LOT OF LOOSE FUR TO GROW
INTO. TWO WEEKS LATER (BELOW), IT HAS
BALLOONED INTO A ROTUND CHERUB, AND
CONTINUES TO SUCKLE ON ITS MOTHER'S
RICH MILK. THREE WEEKS AFTER BIRTH
(RIGHT), THE PUP HAS GROWN LARGE
ENOUGH TO BE WEANED. SUDDENLY, IT
FINDS ITSELF ALONE ON THE BEACH. IN
VAIN, IT SEARCHES FOR ITS MOTHER WHO
HAS LEFT TO FEED AT SEA. FROM NOW ON,
THE PUP WILL HAVE TO FEND FOR ITSELF.
ENDOWED WITH 260 POUNDS (120 KG) OF
PUPPY FAT, IT IS WELL PREPARED FOR
LEANER TIMES, UNTIL IT LEARNS HOW TO
HUNT AT SEA.

At birth, an elephant seal pup's head and tail appear disproportionately large for its tiny, shrivelled body. A loose coat of velvety black fur hangs in pleats around its little body. The pup will suckle on milk richer even than that of whales, and before long, its belly will bulge like a ripe watermelon, filling out the folds of its oversized birth coat. As the days go by, the pup's pitch-black fur gradually fades, from the belly outward, to a dark shade of gray.

During this period the mother and pup undergo a staggering transformation: the pup gains nine pounds (4 kg) a day, while the mother loses over twice as much weight. Almost half of her daily weight loss is transformed directly into puppy fat. Within three weeks the pup will have tripled its original birth weight of ninety pounds (40 kg). After suckling her pup for approximately three weeks, his mother will abruptly abandon it and swim away for good.

What most differentiates the Valdés Peninsula from other elephant seal colonies is that three-quarters of the 125 miles (200 km) of shoreline is ideal for breeding, making it the most spread-out rookery in the world. Elephant seals are known to prefer spacious sand or pebble beaches, but ideal breeding space is often restricted. In the crowded sub-Antarctic rookeries, where the elephant seals lie head to tail, almost a quarter of the pups are trampled to death or otherwise killed before they are weaned. The small, dispersed harems at the Valdés Peninsula dramatically increase the chances for their survival. Physical contact between animals is rare and females are less frequently aggressive toward alien pups. Fewer pups risk

Above and left: ADULT BULLS TEND TO IGNORE THE LITTLE BLACK PUPS, SO AS LONG AS THEY ARE NOT IN THEIR WAY, THE PUPS ARE RELATIVELY SAFE. PUP MORTALITY AT THE VALDÉS PENINSULA IS CONSIDERABLY LOWER (4.4 PERCENT) THAN AMONG THE CRAMPED ROOKERIES OF THE SUB-ANTARCTIC ISLANDS, WHERE THERE IS A GREATER CHANCE OF BEING CRUSHED TO DEATH BY A MASSIVE BEACHMASTER. AN ESTIMATED 60 PERCENT OF THE PENINSULA'S 12,000 PUPS LIVE THROUGH THEIR FIRST YEAR.

Opposite: AFTER HAVING BEEN ABANDONED BY THEIR MOTHERS, THESE CHUBBY GRAY PUPS SEEK COMFORT AND COMPANY FROM FELLOW WEANERS.

getting displaced and lost in the chaos of the colony, and fewer are trampled to death or smothered by rampaging bulls.

The number of pups born at the Valdés Peninsula has increased 150 percent between 1975 and 1992. Pup mortality there is among the lowest in the world, less than 5 percent. With an average of 12,000 births a year, it is the fourth largest rookery in the world. Sadly, despite this, rising numbers of tourists are affecting the breeding behavior in some of the rookeries at Valdés. Biologists have reported that in certain areas where tourists descend to the beach, more females are prematurely abandoning their pups. In January 1998, a bull elephant seal was found shot dead, next to a badly wounded female. The perpetrators were never found. The limited resources available to the local park service and the large size of the peninsula make policing the coast a difficult task.

Whalers have traditionally been a threat to elephant seals, because after whale stocks were depleted, they turned to the seals for commercial resources. Because this species yielded far more oil than any other type of seal, they were killed in devastating numbers on the circumpolar islands. The southern elephant seal population has diminished markedly since the nineteenth century. At the Valdés Peninsula, several thousand animals were culled between 1916 and 1953. Although they have not been hunted since 1964, elephant seals remain vulnerable wherever their interests conflict with those of humans. Once again, the fate of this strange and fascinating animal is at the mercy of man.

Pages 74–75: AFTER THE BREEDING SEASON, IN LATE DECEMBER, A SMALL GROUP OF FEMALES AND JUVENILE MALES GATHER ON A SANDY BEACH NEAR PUNTA HERCULES TO BEGIN THEIR ANNUAL MOLT.

Left: THE VALDÉS PENINSULA IS THE MOST SPREAD-OUT BREEDING AREA IN THE WORLD, OFFERING THE MOST SPACE FOR INDIVIDUALS AND HAREMS. A SUCCESSFUL BEACHMASTER AT VALDÉS MAY BE ABLE TO GATHER OVER 130 FEMALES, BUT SMALL HAREMS OF ABOUT A DOZEN ARE THE AVERAGE. THE FARTHER APART HIS FEMALES, THE TOUGHER IT IS FOR A BEACHMASTER TO KEEP THEM UNDER CONTROL, AND THE EASIER IT BECOMES FOR OUTSIDERS TO SNEAK IN AND SNAG A COW. AS A RESULT, THE PENINSULA'S HAREMS TEND TO BE SMALLER THAN IN OTHER PLACES, WHILE MORE MALES THAN USUAL CAN ENJOY THE SPOILS OF FATHERHOOD.

Opposite: BATTLES AMONG ALPHA MALES OF EQUAL SIZE AND STRENGTH CAN BE BRUTAL AND LENGTHY. AS THE BULLS CHASE EACH OTHER DOWN THE BEACH, THE FIGHT FOR SUPREMACY CONTINUES IN THE SHALLOWS IN FRONT OF THE ROOKERY.

Orca (ORCINUS ORCA)

Cunning Strategies

As I stepped out of the cabin, a gust of wind whirled a cloud of fine sand into my face. I zipped up my windbreaker and headed for the edge of the cliff, where the gales blew so strongly I had to sit down to steady myself. Dangling my legs over the edge, I looked over the vast expanse of whitewashed sea below.

On days like these, it was practically impossible to identify the spout of a right whale among the whitecaps before it would blow away. But then, just ahead, the head of a right whale broke out of a wave. Though right whales are ponderous swimmers, this one appeared to be moving quickly, almost frantically. I wondered whether the current was driving it too close to the treacherous sand banks at the mouth of Caleta Valdés, where two right whales had been stranded just months ago.

Suddenly, the large triangular fin of an orca emerged in front of the right whale's head. Then, two smaller fins appeared to its left. The whale abruptly changed course and headed out to deeper water, boring through the waves like a bulldozer. But the orcas zig-zagged in front of it, cutting off its path. From the shapes of their fins and saddle patches, I soon recognized Ishtar, a large adult female from the local pod of orcas, and two young orcas, Jasmine and tiny Tania.

Turning sharply, Ishtar maneuvered herself onto the right whale's head. Terrified, it lifted its tail and dove away. Minutes later, it resurfaced. Immediately Ishtar swam back on top of its head—clearly she was trying to block the right whale's blowholes to deprive it of air, an assault move designed to kill it. Natural mimics, the two juniors soon followed suit. They took turns as they rode and rolled on top of its body, as if they were scratching their bellies on its callosities. Whenever the right whale surfaced, an orca would already be draped over its enormous head like a headband. It was a sorry sight.

The youngsters continued the chase, Ishtar swimming right next to them, as if watching over the playful progress of this next generation of future hunters. Then, some twenty minutes into the game, she unexpectedly led her protégés away, letting the right whale go unharmed.

UNLIKE THE SNOUTS OF SEALS AND SEA LIONS, THE NOSE OF WHALES AND DOLPHINS HAS MIGRATED TO THE TOP OF THEIR HEAD. WHILE RIGHT WHALES RETAIN TWO NOSTRILS IN THE FORM OF FORKED SLITS, THEY HAVE FUSED INTO A SINGLE BLOWHOLE IN ORCAS AND OTHER DOLPHINS. NO LONGER ABLE TO SMELL, THEY HAVE DEVELOPED A NEW, EXTREMELY SOPHISTICATED SENSE: THAT OF ECHOLOCATION, OR HIGH-FREQUENCY SONAR CLICKS.

There is nothing in the sea that is potentially safe from a hungry orca, or killer whale—they can prey on large whales, other members of their fellow dolphin family, rays, turtles, birds, and even white sharks. "Killer whale," however, is a misleading name, for these beautiful animals are neither whales nor wanton killers. They are the largest and most majestic members of the dolphin family, and like lions or wolves, must hunt to survive. This name merely reflects their qualities as a formidable predator at the crest of the marine food chain.

Orcas are agile like dolphins, can bite like sharks, and are among the ocean's fastest creatures, maneuvering at speeds of up to thirty-four miles (55 km) per hour. As the supreme predator in the sea, they are known to dine on twenty-nine species of fish, fourteen types of pinnipeds, nine types of penguins, and twenty-two members of their own cetacean family. They have even been seen attacking caribou and elk when swimming across stretches of water. The orca is a cunning predator, known to successfully attack much larger whales—even blue whales, which can grow to almost 100 feet (30 m) long. At the Valdés Peninsula, there have been several trying encounters between orcas and right whale mothers and calves. The females protect their calves by forming a circle around them, thrashing the sea to a foamy white with their massive tails. Single whales are occasionally harassed by orcas swimming over their flippers and back, or crisscrossing in front of their noses. No actual attack on a right whale has ever been witnessed, although a few stranded right whale calves have been found with what appeared to be bite marks from orcas.

The orca's ability to exploit a vast variety of prey has allowed it to adapt to all kinds of marine environments, making it the most cosmopolitan of all marine mammals. While it tends to prefer the cooler waters of higher latitudes, the orca can be found in all of the world's oceans, although its total population is unknown.

Along the coasts of British Columbia and Washington State, where resident orcas have been studied since the early 1970s, the family life of these remarkably sociable animals has been well documented. An orca spends its entire life inside the whale clan into which it was born. Females form the backbone of an orca society. A pod is a multigenerational family unit, led by an old female or grandmother who, with a life span of up to eighty years, tends to be most experienced. Males, on the other hand, are believed to reach a maximum age of fifty or sixty years.

Female orcas are believed to be able to reproduce between eleven and forty-five years of age. A birth rate of not more than four or five single calves throughout a female's life ensures a long period of nurturing and development for her offspring. Post-reproductive grandmothers, aunts, and older siblings all take an active part in caring for and teaching the youngest members of the pod.

Orcas mature slowly. Many aspects of their behavior are not genetically encoded, but are learned over time and are passed on from one generation to the next—such as the unique vocal repertoire or "dialect" which distinguishes each orca family, their knowledge of their underwater terrain and of different types of prey, as well as their hunting techniques.

Hunting Strategies

The hunting strategies of these highly adaptable predators vary enormously, depending on what type of prey they are pursuing. In the Antarctic Peninsula, orcas regularly bump ice floes to tip seals and pen-

guins into the water. Or they may perform a coordinated leap, creating a huge wave that washes their prey into the water, where they become easy snacks.

In Norway, they follow migrating schools of herring into the fjords, where they encircle them and drive them together by flashing the panicked fish with their white bellies. Sometimes they trap the herring by driving them against the surface. Once the bait ball is tight enough, the orcas take turns at smacking the fish with their huge, powerful tails, creating loud underwater explosions. In this torrent of silvery scales, each member of the pod takes turns at picking up the stunned or dead herrings.

Orcas are such specialized hunters that in the Pacific Northwest, two separate groups have evolved to exploit different types of prey in the same area. The resident orcas follow spawning salmon like a long drift net, corralling the fish into coves or against rocks or other underwater barriers. The transient group, on the other hand, specializes in capturing warm-blooded marine mammals such as dolphins, porpoises, and seals. On several occasions, transient orcas have been observed chasing Dall's porpoises by leaping clear of the water for several body lengths at a time.

The differences in behavioral skills not only reflect the orcas' adaptation to available food resources, but also influence the size and structure of orca society. Marine mammal hunters, for example,

Opposite: ORCAS EXHALE UNDER WATER, TO REDUCE TIME SPENT AT THE SURFACE, WHICH ALLOWS THEM TO SNATCH A BREATH OF AIR, AS THEY BRUSH THE SURFACE, IN A TINY FRACTION OF A SECOND.

Right: FEMALES AND CALVES FORM THE BACKBONE OF ORCA SOCIETY. ORCA CALVES NURSE FOR TWO YEARS, BUT THE BOND WITH THEIR MOTHERS LASTS A LIFETIME. BOTH MALE AND FEMALE OFFSPRING USUALLY REMAIN IN THE POD INTO WHICH THEY WERE BORN, CREATING EXTENDED ORCA FAMILIES ALONG MATRILINEAL LINES. THE FEMALES MATE WITH MALES FROM OTHER FAMILIES, THUS ORCA FATHERS LIVE IN A DIFFERENT POD THAN THEIR CALVES.

seem to be more efficient when cooperating in tight groups of two to seven individuals. They produce fewer calves than their fish-eating cousins, which live in tightly knit family units that can number several dozen individuals.

The orcas that specialize in feeding on fish communicate and coordinate their complex hunting maneuvers through an elaborate vocabulary of whistles, squeals, and shrieks, since fish are not alerted by their calls. Marine mammals, on the other hand, possess excellent hearing, so the orca must stalk them in relative silence. The orcas use few calls and rely mainly on sonar clicks to assess the position of the other members of their pod. Only immediately after a kill does the sea explode with their triumphant cries.

The Valdés Orcas

Although the Valdés orcas feed on fish and occasionally gulp down a penguin, their favorite quarry on this remote Patagonian outpost are the many seals and sea lions that migrate to the peninsula's shore to breed and bear their young. It remains unclear whether the peninsula's orcas are part of the same pod or whether the small groups traveling together are splinter groups or sub-pods. It is also unknown whether, as in other parts of the world, they live in matriarchal societies. The strict social structure of the salmon-hunting resident whales does not apply to the Valdés orcas. Interestingly, it is the adult bulls that seem to divide the peninsula's waters into territorial spheres of influence. They respectfully stay clear of each other, while all other whales appear to mingle freely.

In many ways the Valdés orcas behave much like the marine-mammal hunting transient orcas, for which group composition is directly related to the needs of reproduction and efficient hunting. The ideal

pod size for transient whales is three individuals: an adult cow, her eldest son, and another offspring. Once the pod exceeds that number, the eldest daughter or youngest offspring may disperse, but daughters usually return to their mothers to give birth. The pod of five, then, is of the right size to take turns hunting and babysitting.

When the calf has become an effective hunter, the daughter may leave again, until she returns to deliver her next calf. Solitary males have also been reported. These may occasionally travel with others and sometimes two groups may join temporarily to hunt larger prey.

Much like the transient whales, the Valdés orcas travel alone or in small groups of varying size and composition. Sometimes solitary males, such as those named Des and Mel, travel in the company of other whales, and occasionally as many as nine orcas will hunt together. Groups of five or seven whales that

include calves are common. And like transient whales, the Valdés orcas are quiet hunters that travel silently so as not to alert the sensitive ears of any potential prey.

Intentional Beaching

To capture elephant seals and sea lions, this pod of orcas has developed an extraordinary hunting technique that literally takes them to the limits of their aquatic environment: they snatch their hapless prey right off the beach. The orcas catapult themselves through shallow water and onto the shore, breaking out of the waves with open jaws to capture startled elephant seals and sea lions. Momentarily stranded, with thrashing prey in their mouths, they wait for a second wave to ride back to the safety of deeper waters.

Although cornering a seal against the beach in a surprise attack may be highly effective, hunting in an alien environment is risky and can be potentially fatal for the orcas. The orcas at Valdés have the advantage of steeply sloping beaches that enable them to slide with relative ease back into the sea. There has been only one known occasion of a beaching at the peninsula. In 1989, two orcas, known as Sparky and Nadia, became stuck on the Punta Norte reef while pursuing sea lions. As the tide went out they were completely stranded on the rocks. For many hours, ranger Roberto García-Vera and a group of tourists kept the animals wet until the tide returned and they were able to swim to safety.

Five thousand miles (8,000 km) farther to the east, in the Crozet Islands of the Indian Ocean, the only other group of orcas in the world to use this unusual technique has been less fortunate. The shoreline is more level and consequently more dangerous,

Above: DEEP INSIDE CALETA VALDÉS, I WATCHED TWO ORCAS COURTING AND MATING. IN A SENSUAL AQUATIC BALLET, THEIR LARGE BODIES WIGGLED AND ROLLED AS THEY PLOUGHED THROUGH THE SWELLS, BRUSHING UP AGAINST EACH OTHER. FOLLOWING JUST BEHIND THE FEMALE, THE MALE GENTLY BUTTED HIS HEAD AGAINST HER GENITAL REGION. THE FEMALE ROLLED ON HER SIDE, HER VENTRAL AREA FACING THE MALE. SWIMMING IN TANDEM, THEIR BELLIES STRADDLED EACH OTHER, UNTIL THEY SLOWLY SLIPPED UNDER THE SURFACE.

Opposite: DURING THE AUSTRAL SPRING, THE BREEDING SEASON OF THE SOUTHERN ELEPHANT SEAL, THE ORCAS PATROL THE SHORES OF CALETA VALDÉS IN SEARCH OF WEANER PUPS AND MOLTING YEARLINGS THAT SNOOZE ALONG THE WATER'S EDGE. AFTER A SUCCESSFUL HUNT, THE WHALES OFTEN GLIDE ALONG THE INLET'S BANKS, RUBBING THEIR STOMACHS AND FLANKS AGAINST THE LARGE ROUND PEBBLES, WHICH SEEMS TO PRODUCE A PLEASURABLE, MASSAGE-LIKE SENSATION.

Orca Hunts

As the tide reached its peak, five orcas entered the large circular bay at the mouth of the inlet. Like huge triangular blades, their black dorsal fins sliced silently through the glistening water. The whales formed a line, rising and sinking as they surfaced, to breathe and dove in complete synchronicity.

Two elephant seal yearlings who had come to the inlet to shed their skins engaged in endless mock fights. They barked and shuffled in chases, sending rivulets of rounded black pebbles into the swelling stream, unaware that this might be alerting their predators of their presence. Hugging the deeper outer edge of the inlet, the orcas reached a crescent-shaped bay dotted with obese gray elephant seals. Too large to enter the shallow waters of the bay, one male orca positioned himself at its mouth, while four smaller orcas separated into two groups and swam in. They passed within a few feet of a snoring bull, who slept oblivious to his brush with fate, and headed straight to a small cluster of slumbering weaners on a bluff near the water's edge.

Within seconds the sea exploded as two orcas broke out of the water, crashing headlong into the tight group of weaners. Clenching their jaws firmly around the little tails of two struggling, yapping pups, the whales pulled them slowly but steadily toward the water. One pup then broke free and plunged into the waves but was swiftly snatched by one of the other orcas patrolling deeper waters, ready to block just such an escape. With their catch safely between their teeth, and trailed by a flock of greedy gulls, the group headed out to rejoin the old bull and share their meal.

THE PENINSULA'S TIDES ARE CRUCIAL TO
THE ORCA'S HUNTING SUCCESS. ONLY AT
HIGH TIDE CAN THEY SWIM THROUGH THE
CHANNELS IN THE EXTENDED REEFS THAT
PROTECT *PUNTA NORTE'S* SEA LION ROOK-
ERIES, AND THEY HAVE JUST A FEW HOURS
TO PATROL *CALETA VALDÉS* BETWEEN
TIDES. AT *CALETA VALDÉS,* THE ORCAS
MUST WAIT FOR WATERS TO RISE TO NAVI-
GATE ACROSS THE TREACHEROUS SAND-
BANKS AT THE SOUND'S ENTRANCE. *MOST*
ELEPHANT SEALS SLEEP ABOVE THE TIDE-
MARK, SO IF THE WHALES WANT TO SNATCH
A SEAL OFF THE BEACH, THEY CAN ONLY DO
SO CLOSE TO HIGH TIDE.

and a number of whales have become stranded along its treacherous coasts.

The Orca's Hunting Grounds

As in other parts of the world, much of the orca's activity at Valdés coincides with the seasonal availability and movements of its prey. The highest concentration of accessible sea lion colonies can be found at Punta Norte, where they breed during the austral summer. Caleta Valdés is a favorite haunt for elephant seals, from the beginning of their breeding season in September through the end of the molting season in late February.

This narrow, river-like inlet winds along twenty-two miles (35 km) of the peninsula's eastern tip and is flanked by a long tongue of gravel, which protects it from the crushing waves of the South Atlantic. Caleta Valdés has the calmest waters on the peninsula, providing refuge to hundreds of elephant seals that snooze along its gravel banks or frolic in the many tidal pools that dot the landscape. But the peaceful turquoise waters and rolling pebbled shores are deceptively safe, since unlike most other breeding grounds in the area, they lack the wide protective reefs to defend the fledgling elephant seal population from the threat of marauding orcas. As the tide rises, the water edges closer to the orca's favorite prey: the motley gray elephant seal weaner pups, round and fattened on their mother's rich, oily milk.

As the elephant seal season nears its end and more and more animals leave to forage the rich waters above the continental shelf break, the orcas appear more frequently to hunt at Punta Norte, some thirty miles (50 km) north of Caleta Valdés. This tip of land, on the northernmost flank of the peninsula, lies to the east of the small, bean-shaped Gulf of San José and faces the open waters of the enormous Gulf of San Matías. A four-mile (6-km) stretch of beach along the windswept coast is home to a number of southern sea lion colonies.

During the last days of December, these rookeries begin to grow with the return of plump, pregnant females. Greeted by rampant bulls eager to dominate them, the females are soon incorporated in one of the many harems. A few days after their arrival, when the summer temperatures peak in early January, they give birth to tiny, coal-black pups.

By March the pups, now a couple months old, begin to venture into the sea. Soon the coast is teeming with cavorting, inquisitive youngsters taking their first clumsy excursions into the fluid medium that will soon become their home. Protected by a wide reef that protrudes far into the sea, they seem safe as they frolic in the shallow green tidal pools between the rocks. But the barrier separating the colonies from the sea is split by a number of crevasses that bring the open ocean uncomfortably close to the rookery, especially at high tide. For the orcas patrolling along the coast, these channels provide a unique opportunity to swim right up to the beach.

There is nothing more difficult or dangerous for an orca than to strand itself on the beach while capturing a seal. To home in on a tiny pup, at the right spot and moment, requires perfect timing and coordination. It is far easier for an orca to launch itself ashore by riding a wave than it is to push its hefty body back to sea once it has lost all buoyancy. For an orca to return to deeper water requires a considerable amount of agility and strength, and demands incredible control over its massive body. From an early age, an orca is taught this dangerous hunting technique, and even the most experienced hunters practice regularly on a gradually sloping beach in the Bay of Medina.

Opposite: AMBUSHES OCCUR ONLY AT HIGH TIDE, WHEN THE ORCAS CAN SWIM RIGHT UP TO THE BEACH, WHICH IS NORMALLY PROTECTED BY EXTENSIVE REEFS. TO REDUCE THE CHANCE OF GETTING WASHED UP BY HIGH WAVES, THEY ATTACK ONLY ON RELATIVELY WINDLESS DAYS. IF ALL OF THESE CONDITIONS COME TOGETHER, EVERY THIRD ATTACK ENDS IN SUCCESS.

Below: ALTHOUGH THEY HAVE BEEN HUNTED HERE FOR MANY GENERATIONS, SEA LIONS FROM THE NEARBY COLONY NONETHELESS APPEAR TO BE MAGICALLY DRAWN TO THE FAR SIDE OF THE ATTACK CHANNEL. STILL, THEY ARE AWARE OF THE DANGER OF ORCA ATTACKS, AND THE OLDER ANIMALS BOB UP AND DOWN IN THE SURF CRANING THEIR NECKS FOR ANY TRIANGULAR FINS PATROLLING THE SHORELINE. THEN AT SOME INVISIBLE SIGN THEY SPEED UP AND PORPOISE QUICKLY ACROSS THE CRACK IN THE REEF, ONLY TO RETURN A LITTLE WHILE LATER.

Watching Mel

Just as the tide was beginning to rise, Mel, Punta Norte's solitary orca bull, slowly made his way along the three-mile (5-km) stretch of coastline between the Bay of Medina and the attack channel. Those of us who had not yet taken our places in one of the three blinds on the beach ran as fast as we could along the narrow path between the thornbushes. If Mel arrived at the channel before we did, we would not be allowed to descend to the beach.

We peeked over the sand dunes, making sure that none of the sea lions from the nearby rookery were aware of our approach, which might trigger a stampede into the water and straight into the open jaws of a waiting orca. Assured that we hadn't been noticed, we crawled the last two hundred feet (60 m) to the blinds, our bulky backpacks and heavy photographic equipment slowing our progress. We had to push ourselves through the scorching sand on our bellies like a commando of military storm-troopers.

Mel's timing was like clockwork. An hour into the rising tide, he was circling at the mouth of the channel, about 325 feet (100 m) offshore. Soon the 160-foot- (50-m-) wide crevasse in the reef would fill with enough water to allow the massive bull safe passage between the rocky outcrops.

Curious and carefree, the tiny black pups followed the rest of the herd into the water. Hopping along the shore, they ducked into the surf, only to be rolled around and spewed back onto the beach. The innocent youngsters had no clue of the danger threatening their lives. The emerald swells bore a sinister presence that was lured by their clumsy splashes.

Mel hid in the depths of the channel, swimming sideways to conceal his five-foot- (1.6-m-) tall dorsal fin. We could only see his long shadow trailing the unsuspecting seals as they swam across the channel, sometimes just six to nine feet (2 to 3 m) away, but nothing happened. The tension in the blinds was nerve-wracking. From time to time he would come up for air, deliberately swimming away to deceive the older seals.

Four hours later, he still had not caught a single animal. The tide was receding, and the first rocks were beginning to show. Mel was milling about in deeper waters outside the channel. From the blind next door came a whisper: "That's it for today; let's start packing up and get out of here as silently as possible," said Hector Cassín, the wildlife inspector. The mood among the photographers and filmakers was somber.

Just as I was dismantling my tripod, I heard a whistle. All around me people were shuffling and scrambling about, and for a moment I did not understand what was going on. Someone kicked me, and I looked toward the water. Several seals were swimming leisurely along the shore. Suddenly, a large wall-like wave thundered toward us. Crashing with full force onto the beach, it parted, revealing Mel's enormous black and white body. Dangling between his huge conical teeth was a tiny black pup. His tall dorsal fin shook violently as he bashed the pup against the pebbles, shaking it from side to side to separate the flesh from the hide. Then he flexed his body and turned broadside. With powerful beats of his tail, he slowly inched through the shallows until an incoming wave lifted him back out to sea. For a long time we watched him circling far out in deeper waters, trailed by flocks of gulls and petrels who were greedily waiting for leftovers.

Cooperative Hunting Techniques

Toward the end of the season I had the opportunity to witness quite a different hunting spectacle. A group of eight orcas, which only occasionally visit Punta Norte, spent several days in the area. When hunting in pairs or as a group, orcas cooperate much like a pride of

lions or a pack of wolves, and always share their catch. Their impressive coordinated attacks are marked by a strict division of labor, each member playing a specific role. One of this group's favorite hunting strategies was for a larger whale to act as a decoy, sailing past the sea lions in full view while the others engaged in a sneak attack.

There were several younger whales, which because of their smaller size were able to access the more shallow areas above the reef. They could also take sea lions much closer to shore without having to beach themselves as much as giant Mel had to.

Another tactic was for the smaller orcas to patrol the reefs on either side of the attack channel, cutting off the sea lions' escape route to shallow water above the rocks. Others would form a wall in deeper water to keep the prey from fleeing toward the open ocean. A third group would swim sideways, flashing their white bellies, to herd the sea lions together. Corralled inside the channel or against the beach, the hapless animals were usually captured by one or two of the older and more experienced hunters. Then, as if to celebrate their success, the orcas played with their catch like big cats toying with a tiny mouse.

One afternoon I watched Sparky, one of the adult females, drag off a plump yearling. In an explosion of foam, she breached victoriously, her victim helplessly locked between her jaws. Then she let the seal go. As it desperately tried to swim away, Sparky swam up to it and delivered a loud sideways smack with her paddle-like flipper that sent the seal flying through a cloud of spray. A second, explosive blow with her large tail catapulted the seal so high into the air that it soared with outstretched flippers among the petrels and gulls waiting for scraps. As soon as it hit the surface, she snapped it up again, towing it farther offshore, where the kill was finally shared with the rest of the pod. A cloud of

scavenging birds swooped into the water around the milling orcas. A red oily slick on the surface was all that remained.

Training Sessions

About a third of all attacks on seals occur in the water, where the capture is complicated by the vast number of escape routes available. Expertise is born of training, and only the most experienced hunters succeed. To survive, the orcas must practice their hunting skills. At Punta Norte and Caleta Valdés they regularly stage training sessions in open-sea hunting.

Orca Sports

Every day, during low tide, and in the absence of prey, several members of the pod would travel to the Bay of Medina, several miles north of the attack channel. There they would strand themselves simultaneously, all in a neat row, about ten feet (3 m) apart from each other. Arching their backs and lifting their flukes, they would spend a few motionless seconds on the beach before wiggling their way out to sea with great thumps of their tails. A few minutes later they would return, only to repeat the exhausting process, which, depending on the tides, could last an entire morning or afternoon.

Seals would sometimes be slightly disabled by a more experienced whale and then released to be recaptured by the younger members of the pod. Again and again, sea lions would be set free, just to be snapped up moments later by one of the young whales. They would often taunt and maul them, bumping them with their blunt snouts, grabbing them by the folds in their skin, lifting them out of the water, or dragging them underwater by their tails.

One time I saw a wild, playful race take place with all younger members of the pod chasing the main

AN ORCA BREACHES TRIUMPHANTLY,
HOLDING ITS HAPLESS VICTIM FIRMLY
BETWEEN ITS TEETH. IN A VIOLENT
SHOW OF FORCE IT TOSSES THE SEAL
THROUGH THE AIR BEFORE DROWNING
AND EATING IT.

hunter, prey in mouth, while attempting to snatch his catch. Finally, with a light flick of its head, the adult orca flung the seal to one of the calves, as if playing some kind of ball game. The next day an unsuspecting penguin was caught and released as a live training target for the budding hunters.

Orcas and Their Prey

There is no doubt that the orca's enormous body needs a large amount of food to maintain its energy levels. It is believed that orcas need to consume between 2.5 and 5 percent of their body weight a day. For a seven-ton whale about the size of Mel, that would be equivalent to an average of one adult sea lion, a female elephant seal, or four to five small sea lion pups a day.

At Punta Norte, one out of five of the four hundred pups born each season fall prey to the orcas within three months. Nevertheless, the orca's impact on the peninsula's marine mammal population is negligible. For all their notoriety, very few orcas patrol the peninsula's shores. Their diet is made up of a variety of prey. Likewise, the peninsula's nineteen orcas pose no threat to a growing population of 19,000 sea lions and 43,000 elephant seals.

Setbacks

In 1977, the government of the neighboring province of Rio Negro ordered the extinction of all orcas visiting the sea lion rookery at Punta Bermeja. This was due to the unrealistic belief that they were consuming up to one hundred sea lions a day, eradicating the main local tourist attraction. Both Mel and his ten-year older brother, Bernd, had then been targeted by a special firing squad. Sensing the danger, the orcas

swam to safety and not a single whale was killed, but Mel's crooked dorsal fin still bears testimony to a bullet wound. The brothers survived, but since Mel's dorsal fin was not yet fully developed, it continued to grow with a marked inclination to the right. In 1992, old Bernd was shot again, this time by two mindless youths, which added two new holes to his jagged dorsal fin. Ironically, today, the same orcas have become the most sought-after sight by visitors from all over the world who hope to catch a glimpse of the notorious hunting technique.

Compared to other parts of the world—as in British Columbia, where orcas are counted by the hundreds, or in Iceland, by the thousands—the Patagonian population is very small, and until recently their numbers were thought to be declining.

Unlike seals and right whales, orcas were never commercially hunted. There are no known reasons for why there are such few orcas in northern Patagonia, where there would certainly be enough resources to sustain larger populations.

In the mid-1970s, twenty-six orcas in the waters off the Valdés Peninsula had been identified by the distinctive markings of their saddle patches, and the shape and size of their dorsal fins. But by the mid-1980s, only seventeen individuals were known to local researchers (though a population of about thirty had been estimated). During the early 1990s, the situation seemed to be worsening for the small population of Valdés orcas who inhabit an area of 15,000 square miles (40,000 sq. km) between the mouth of the Rio Negro in the north, to slightly beyond the Valdés Peninsula in the south.

Ruby, an exceptionally avid hunter, developed a tumor, and was last seen in 1991. By that time a large tumor-like growth had also formed on the head of Bernd. Together with his advancing age, the tumor

An Act of Mercy

O ne day at dawn, I had a most memorable experience. When I got to the blind, the sun was
still under the horizon, but its first tentacles
were already stretching across the sky tinting the thin,
streaky clouds in pale shades of rose.

Mel was swimming back and forth inside the attack
channel. Just as the rising sun began to bathe everything
pink, three sea lion pups clumsily hopped and paddled
through the surf along the beach. Accelerating like a
powerboat, Mel surfed in on a wave, swiftly snapping up
one of the pups. It was so tiny that it disappeared
entirely inside Mel's mouth. As always, he immediately
turned sideways and wiggled his way out to sea. There
he circled briefly, then swam slowly back to shore. At the
beach, he opened his mouth, and the pup fell out onto
the sand. With unbelievable tenderness and care, giant,
fearsome Mel nudged the tiny fellow up the beach with
his snout until the startled pup wobbled away into the
morning light.

I watched the pup for a while, but it appeared
unharmed and healthy. We cannot judge other species by
human standards, and shall never fully comprehend
their actions. Yet I wondered for a long time whether
Mel had been playing, sharpening his hunting skills, or
whether this had been a true act of mercy.

ORCAS DO NOT ALWAYS CAPTURE TO KILL.
OCCASIONALLY PUPS ARE SEIZED JUST TO BE
RELEASED AGAIN A FEW MOMENTS LATER.
THE ORCAS HANDLE THEM WITH ASTONISH-
ING GENTLENESS AND CARE AND THE PUPS
APPEAR TO BE COMPLETELY UNHARMED.

may have impaired his effectiveness as the principal hunter, for in Bernd's latter years, Mel took over the lead. When Bernd was last seen in the autumn of 1993, he was presumed to be at least forty years old.

Bernd's disappearance caused widespread concern for Mel, who became the sole hunter at Punta Norte, apart from occasional stints by other orcas. A type of ulcer grew on his jaw, believed to be a painful bone infection, and a slight depression behind his blowhole was thought to be a sign of malnutrition. During the seasons following Bernd's death, Mel's behavior grew increasingly erratic. Although he regularly visited the traditional attack channel, he spent most of his time milling about, half-heartedly following some seal, only to abort his pursuit a few moments later. Rarely did he engage in an actual attack.

Anxious researchers began tracking Mel's movements twenty-four hours a day, and found that he hunted on moonlit nights. This sparked a controversy as to whether the increasing number of scientists, film teams, and photographers, all of whom spend the entire season in blinds on the beach in the traditional attack areas, were disturbing the sea lion communities. Indeed, the number of seals crossing the channel had decreased, and they frequently seemed alarmed, peering at the blinds on the beach.

Was the prey available to Mel decreasing due to human intrusion, or was Mel just becoming old and frail? If Mel disappeared, who would take his place at Punta Norte, and continue the amazing and unique technique that has made these orcas so famous around the world?

Luckily, the situation improved, thanks to the birth of five new calves in the 1990s. Jasmine, the most intrepid of all the young hunters, was born in the early nineties, followed by little Tania, who was first seen in 1994. Tiny Yaco was born in 1996, while two more new babies appeared in late 1997 and early 1998. The older calves already are beaching themselves to hunt seals and sea lions, continuing this unique and rare tradition. Despite fears for the worst, Mel is alive and well, and continues to hunt successfully. Today, despite some deaths and disappearances, nineteen healthy orcas patrol the peninsula's shores.

ORCA BULLS MAY GROW TO OVER THIRTY FEET (9 M) IN LENGTH AND WEIGH UP TO NINE TONS. THE MORE SLENDER FEMALES RARELY GROW LARGER THAN TWENTY-THREE FEET (7 M) AND WEIGH OVER FOUR TONS. THE SHAPE AND SIZE OF THE TRIANGULAR DORSAL FIN ALSO DIFFERS BETWEEN MALES AND FEMALES. THE FINS OF ADULT MALES ARE GREATLY EXAGGERATED IN SIZE AND CAN REACH A TOWERING SIX FEET (1.8 M), DWARFING THE SHORTER, MORE SICKLE-SHAPED FIN OF EVEN THE LARGEST FEMALES.

South American Sea Lion (OTARIA FLAVESCENS)

LIKE ITS AFRICAN NAMESAKE, THE ADULT SEA LION MALE CARRIES A THICK, LONG MANE OF COARSE HAIR THAT FALLS FROM HIS FOREHEAD ONTO HIS MASSIVE NECK AND CHEST, AND IT TENDS TO BE LIGHTER THAN THAT ON THE REST OF HIS BODY. THE SEA LION'S ENORMOUS BARREL CHEST AND BROAD HEAD IS SO BULKY THAT ITS HINDQUARTERS APPEAR STRANGELY FEE-BLE. SEA LIONS HAVE DISTINCTIVELY UPTURNED PUG-NOSES, ARE ABOUT EIGHT FEET (2.5 M) LONG AND WEIGH UP TO 770 POUNDS (350 KG). FEMALES ARE MORE EVENLY PROPORTIONED WITH SMALLER HEADS AND NO MANE. THEY ARE ABOUT SIX AND A HALF FEET (2 M) LONG AND WEIGH AROUND 310 POUNDS (140 KG).

Since prehistoric times, the sea lion has been hunted as a dependable food source. Their gregarious habits, tendency to return to the same breeding areas and haul-out sites, and their defenselessness on land make them easy targets. Patagonian and Fuegian Indians traditionally hunted them for food, oil, and pelts. The hides were used to make canoes, rafts, and other objects, while oil and other liquids were stored in sea-lion stomachs.

In the sixteenth century explorers and adventur-ers began hunting them for food and oil. Their oil was utilized for lamp fuel, for tanning cow hides, and to produce soap, while their meat was turned into animal fodder. More recently, they have been hunted commercially to make leather and suede items, and the newborn pups have been used to make coats.

Sealers would creep up on the flanks of a colony and suddenly race toward a herd of sea lions, creating a wild stampede. Then they would drive the wide-eyed animals inland, where they would corner them against cliffs or rocks, cutting off their escape route to the safety of the sea. The sealers then would round up the best individuals, knock them down with a strong blow to the head with a baseball-like bat, and stab the heart with a steel knife on a long pole.

To this day, the skeletons at Punta Norte's "seal cemetery" bear witness to long forgotten slaughters. Rusty cauldrons and oil barrels still line the beach where three to four hundred animals were killed per day. Despite a preference for males, over a quarter of the sea lions culled were females, many of them pregnant. In forty years, almost 270,000 South American sea lions were clubbed to death at the Valdés Peninsula alone, almost as many as today's total estimated world population of approximately three hundred thousands.

The killing of sea lions in Argentina, Chile, and Uruguay, was one of the most extensive slaughters in animal history. Some sixty tons of seal oil were har-vested in 1800. By 1820, it had risen to 2,000 tons per year. In 1876, the great Argentine explorer Francisco Moreno described a sorry sight: "Once upon a time, the coast was a well-known seal hunting ground. Thousands were killed; so many that today one finds

Swimming with Sea Lions

A gentle breeze carried the muffled voices of over two hundred bustling sea lions from the colony across the oyster-shell–shaped bay. Small groups of sea lions porpoising from the rookery were too busy to notice the yellow skiff some hundred feet (30 m) offshore. As soon as we dropped anchor, elongated dark shapes began to shoot through the shallow waters that sparkled in myriad shades of jade. Here and there, shiny wet heads with curly dew-covered whiskers popped through the surface, sneezed, and disappeared.

I quietly slipped down the side of the skiff and peeked into the glassy green. There were no sea lions to be seen. Below me, the sun painted a jigsaw of spider-webs onto the gently swaying seaweed and algae-covered rocks. I let myself float, lulled by the rocking swell, mesmerized by the ever-changing display.

Suddenly, I felt a gentle pull on my right flipper. I jerked around and saw a little beige sea lion swoosh away in terror, leaving behind a trail of pale bubbles. Above the surface, I noticed a half dozen heads bobbing up and down in the waves a yard or so ahead of me. I slowly swam their way, and soon made out a number of shady shapes in the water. Before I knew it, I was surrounded by sea lions. For every head on the surface there were at least three sea lions underwater—twirling, darting, and rolling through the sea with undulating grace. Two well-rounded females twisted their flexible necks to peer backward at me, while they swam straight ahead. Then they flipped over sideways and drifted along right next to me.

Cat-like faces peeked at me with huge dark eyes. There were juveniles and females of all colors, shapes, and sizes. Some were cautious and furtive, others bold. A large mocha-colored female sailed right up to me, pressing her snout against my goggles as if testing them. Other sea lions swirled around in circles, attempting to bark underwater, but blew bubbles instead.

More adventurous sea lions zoomed right up to me, peered into my mask, shot up to the surface for a quick breath, then swiveled back down for another look. All the while, my little beige friend was sneaking up from behind to snatch one of my flippers and nibble at it, ever so gently. I played hide and seek with him for a while. Pretending not to care or notice, I waited until he seized my flipper, then suddenly turned around and watched him dart away. Tiring of the novelty of seeing me in the water, several sea lions began to snooze, their bodies floating below the surface and their noses barely rising above the water.

Suddenly, an enormous black shape shot through the herd. There was instant chaos as the sea lions sped off in all directions. The patriarch had descended from his rock and was herding his females, much as a sheep dog corrals his sheep. Flabbergasted, I watched how he zigzagged back and forth, rounding up every single stray female. All at once, he turned and charged right up to me at incredible speed. He opened his lion-like jaws, blowing huge bubbles, and snapped his sharp teeth shut just inches from my face. I yelled into my snorkel. For an instant I believed he was going to bite my head off, but he swiveled around and shot off, gathering the females ahead of him. Within seconds, I was all alone.

I remembered a warning about mock threat displays by bull sea lions, but I remained shaken. Shivering with fright, and suddenly feeling the cold of spending so much time in the water, I paddled back to the boat.

Contrary to elephant seals, which forage in deep waters 310 miles (500 km) east of the rookery, sea lions travel less than 62 miles (100 km) offshore, remaining on Patagonia's broad continental shelf. Unfortunately, Argentina's expanding coastal fisheries, which operate only a few miles away from some of the major colonies, may be reducing the availability of prey. The jovial sea lions are a thorn to fishermen, who view them as competitors and pests. Their bad habit of following fishing boats repeatedly causes trouble. They feed on netted fish, steal or mutilate catches on hooks, and occasionally damage fishing gear, especially when they get entangled in lines and nets. Although South American sea lions are now officially protected, Peruvian fishermen and Chilean salmon farmers shoot and even dynamite those that come close to their boats and salmon pens.

Opposite and right: IN LATE DECEMBER, THE FIRST LARGE SEA LION BULLS ARRIVE IN THE TRADITIONAL BREEDING AREAS, RESERVING THE MOST COVETED SPOTS, SUCH AS THE ROCKY POINT AT PUNTA PIRÁMIDE. MOST FEMALES ARRIVE IN EARLY JANUARY, AND ARE IMMEDIATELY APPROPRI- ATED BY ONE OF THE MASSIVE BULLS. THEY GIVE BIRTH WITHIN THREE DAYS OF COM- ING TO THE ROOKERY, AND BY THE END OF THE MONTH THE COLONY IS BUSTLING WITH BIG BROWN BULLS, YELLOW FEMALES, AND TINY BLACK PUPS.

Below: OCCASIONALLY SEA LION BULLS PREY ON MAGELLANIC PENGUINS. SCORNING SKIN AND FEATHERS, THEY NEATLY FLAY THEIR QUARRY BY VIOLENTLY SHAKING THEIR HEADS AND BASHING THEM AGAINST THE WATER'S SURFACE.

only small rookeries, as fishermen call the places where sea lions gather."

But the hunt for sea lions was far from over. Between 1917 and 1953 Argentina processed over half a million pelts, and seals were commercially hunted in high numbers through the 1950s. When prices for sea lion leather dropped, the animals continued to be killed for their oil, even though the yield was meager compared to southern elephant seals. By the 1960s, sea lions were losing their economic attraction and hunt- ing declined. Still, by 1974, when Argentina passed laws to protect the South American sea lion, commercial sealing had decimated the country's northern popula- tion by almost 90 percent.

For reasons still little understood, the South American sea lion population is growing at a rate so low it is almost stagnant. There are about 19,000 ani- mals at the Valdés Peninsula, a number which in the past would have been hunted in a single season. Luckily the sea lions are now more valuable as a tourist attraction.

Breeding

At the Valdés Peninsula, the sea lion's breeding season commences with the arrival of the first males and females in mid-December, and lasts through the aus- tral summer months.

Newborn sea lions weigh only about twenty-six pounds (12 kg), about a third as much as elephant seal pups. Sea lion milk is not as rich as that of elephant seals, whose pups grow so rapidly that they can be weaned in just three weeks. Sea lions nurse their young for at least a year, until the next pup is born, and sometimes even beyond that. While elephant seal mothers fast through the nursing period, sea lion cows need to feed regularly. Within a week of giving birth, they return to feed at sea. From now on, the females will forage for three days at a time, returning for two-day nursing stints on land. While their mothers are away, their pups are sheltered inside the rookery, where they play and tumble around together in creches of youngsters. The returning mothers recognize their pups by their bleat and smell, biting and hurling hungry imposters away.

When the first large males arrive in December, they take up positions along the beach in places where the cows are most likely to haul out later in the season. Soon the best positions along the high tide line have been occupied. These territories are guarded vigorously, even before the females arrive, for they are a means of attracting the cows.

Most females will seek the protection of a strong resident bull by settling close to him, but getting there is not always easy. As they haul out on the beach, vagrant males try to intercept their path and drag them away. Although the females violently reject their advances, they must often flee back into the water chased by groups of wayward bachelors, and many are wounded.

Once the females are inside a rookery, they benefit from the protection provided by the resident bulls, which assiduously defend them against idle males. The breeding colony is a refuge, crucial to the survival of their pups. Females that give birth out-

Most females haul out in early January, having fed at sea prior to pupping. The first births occur in the second week of December but almost three-quarters of the pups are born between January 10 and 25, within three days of their mother's arrival at the rookery. Sea lion cows come into heat within a few days of giving birth, and most matings take place in the third week of January, at the peak of the breeding season.

Left: THE PENINSULA'S SEA LIONS RARELY HUNT AT DEPTHS DEEPER THAN 230 FEET (70 M), OR STAY DOWN FOR LONGER THAN SEVEN MINUTES, FOR THE SHALLOW WATERS AROUND VALDÉS TEEM WITH THEIR FAVORITE FOODS: ANCHOVIES, SEA BASS, HAKE, AND SQUID.

Opposite: THE SOUTH AMERICAN SEA LION INHABITS THE PACIFIC AND ATLANTIC COASTS ALONG LATIN AMERICA'S SOUTHERN CONE, FROM PERU TO BRAZIL ALL THE WAY DOWN TO THE ISLANDS AROUND CAPE HORN, AT THE TIP OF THE CONTINENT.

side the protective boundaries of a breeding group risk losing their pups, which may be the reason why they are instinctively drawn to settling near a dominant bull.

Cows that arrive early in the season, before the breeding colonies have formed, are completely outnumbered by competing males. After giving birth and coming into heat, they are heavily disputed over by males trying to mate with them.

The bulls carry females away, leaving their pups behind. Occasionally, one male will forcefully hold a female near him while another holds down her pup. Unable to join their mothers and nurse, the helpless pups starve to death within a few days of being separated. Every December, the first pups born die in this unfortunate manner. The pups of solitary sea lion couples are equally unprotected, and suffer a similar fate. Almost two-thirds of them perish before the end of the breeding season.

But even at the height of the breeding season, inside a bustling rookery, the females and their pups are not entirely safe. With testosterone levels running high, anything seems to trigger a charge by the young bulls lurking around the periphery. The arrival of females attempting to enter the colony, skirmishes among resident males, or blistering summer temperatures, all may precipitate an attack. According to studies conducted at Punta Norte by Claudio Campagna and his colleagues, at peak season groups of peripheral males attack the breeding colony as often as every two hours. Over half of these raids are successfully repelled by the resident bulls, but in the chaos of the ambush, several females get redistributed throughout the rookery. During severe attacks, at least one peripheral male will manage to establish himself inside the breeding aggregation, while another loses all of his females.

Two thirds of the "pirates" are young, subadult males. But despite having strength in numbers, they rarely succeed at kidnapping and holding a female, and almost never get a chance to mate. Not so in the case of adult bulls. In over a third of the raids at least one female is seized by an adult bull. In 15 percent of the cases the adult bull manages to keep a cow captive for several days until she comes into heat and mates with him.

Frustrated by their failure to mate, the impetuous subadults may turn to seizing a pup instead. Almost a quarter of the 400 pups born each season at Punta Norte are sequestered by subadult males during group raids on the breeding colony. Locked out of the ritual breeding, the junior males use the abducted pups as "surrogate" females, defending them against fellow subordinate males, and even mounting them in a brutal charade that may drag on for hours.

Other peripheral males may try to steal the abducted pup, which ends up being grabbed and pulled and jerked around. Luckier pups are dropped and ignored, although they are pinned to the ground as soon as they try to escape. Others are carried out to sea, and some may never make it back to the rookery. Unless an abducted pup can return to its mother, it will die of starvation. Once it manages to scramble away from its kidnapper, it must somehow return to the rookery without being snatched up again by one of the aggressive young males prowling the periphery.

Luckily, almost half of the pups manage to return to the safety of the breeding group before they can be recovered by their tormentors. And despite being bitten and tossed around, the little fellows are sturdier than they appear: only about six percent die, mainly from internal injuries.

The Pirates

*I*t was late January, and the midsummer sun was beating mercilessly from a cloudless sky. I was sitting on a tall sand dune, watching the bustling sea lion colony below, trying to pick out individuals among the pandemonium. There were chocolate-colored bulls with thick, bushy manes and barrel chests surrounded by yellow females. Small pups, their raven coats glistening in the sun, bleated ceaselessly for their mothers. Females barked and snapped at each other. Farther down the beach, sea lions surfed the breakers in front of the colony as they returned from feeding at sea. Were it not for the short explosive hissing sounds made by defensive bulls, the noisy colony would have sounded just like a big herd of sheep.

A group of subadult males bobbed up and down in the surf, craning their necks like periscopes to see what was happening inside the rookery. Several large bulls prowled the periphery of the colony, while others slept in the scorching sand, flippers outstretched to dissipate the heat. As a female attempted to wander off, she was stopped with a brisk body block by the harem bull. One of his neighbors grasped a straying cow and hurled her back into place. If she left his domain it wouldn't be long before a nearby bull incorporated her into his harem, or one of the solitary males dragged her away. Those cows, however, which had given birth and were no longer in heat were free to move in and out of the rookery in order to feed at sea.

By that time, most breeding males had gathered a harem of about four females. Because there were simply not enough cows to go round, the bachelors lurking at the border of the colony were a constant threat. Adult bulls can attack a rookery on their own, attempting to abduct a female or displace a resident bull and settle in his stead. In almost half of these assaults the seasoned bulls are followed by a raucous mob of vagrant subadults and other idle males who gather to form raiding parties of up to forty animals. These pirates storm into the established breeding areas in surprise ambushes to steal the females.

Watching a sea lion rookery is a difficult task if one attempts to be aware of all that is going on. While a female was giving birth at one end, a skirmish erupted between two neighboring bulls at the other. They pranced around each other, hissing nastily. Then one of the contenders charged forward, stopping short just in front of the other bull. Seconds later, the other bull rushed to strike back, but curiously, their bodies never touched. Again and again, they charged at each other, then abruptly stopped and retreated to their starting places. The ritual repeated itself until one of the contenders finally backed off and settled into the sand. Nearby, a tiny black pup clambered over a sleeping bull while his mother called out for it. Finally, she huddled over, gently took the pup into her mouth, and carried it back to safety. Suddenly some two dozen males charged out of the surf. Huffing and puffing, they galloped up the beach and broke into the heart of the rookery. The onslaught of attackers caused havoc inside the colony. Several females bolted away in terror, leaving behind yelping pups, which quickly disappeared among the seething bodies.

The breeding bulls joined forces, racing at the intruders with outstretched necks and open jaws. As they bit and pushed against each other with their bulky chests, a kidnapper grabbed a cow by her neck and abducted her to the periphery of the breeding area, where she was forcefully held captive.

By the time the rookery bulls had rebuffed the intruders, several females had switched territories.

As the cows desperately called for their lost pups, a newly ousted male lay panting on the pebbles at the edge of the rookery. In his place sat a large, reddish bull. Two neighboring males assiduously bit into his hind flippers. He lunged backward, and bit deeply into the first assailant's neck, jerking his head until he drew blood and the resident bull retreated. The remaining male continued to threaten the newcomer, but eventually accepted the new status quo and settled back into the sand.

Page 114: Sea lion bulls that have been unable to establish a harem of their own gang up in raiding parties of four to forty males that attack the breeding colony in an attempt to steal the females. Two thirds of these pirates are young subadult males, not yet strong or experienced enough to breed.

Above: In over half of the aggressive encounters between sea lion bulls, a vocal threat suffices to keep an intruder at bay. In four out of ten clashes, the contest is all bluff. In a strange ritual, the sea lions charge at each other, suddenly stop short, and retreat to their starting places. Fights are usually very brief. They appear violent, but are rarely fatal.

The Threat from Orcas

The early days in the life of a Punta Norte pup are riddled with perils. Having survived forceful separations from its mother and dangerous abductions by ill-tempered bulls, the pup has yet to face its most lethal enemy: the orca, or killer whale.

While Uruguayan sea lions risk being taken in the water by seven gill and smooth hammerhead sharks, the sea lion pups at the Valdés Peninsula are not even safe on shore. The local orcas are daring hunters, and will beach themselves and snatch the succulent youngsters right off their waterfront home. For unknown reasons, the sea lion colonies at Punta Norte migrate south along the coastline. Wide green reefs protect the rookeries from the open ocean, but they are interrupted by several intertidal channels that allow the orcas to swim up to the beach during high tide.

By March, when the two-month-old pups are learning to swim, the first sea lion colony has come within a stone's throw of the largest passage in the reef, the "attack channel." Soon the coast is teeming with inquisitive pups cavorting in the shallows near the rookery. The carefree youngsters attempt to follow their mothers, as they body surf across the waves, and their older cousins, as they porpoise along the coastline. For unknown reasons, the older sea lions are magically drawn to swimming across the attack channel, and the little pups soon follow suit.

But while the more experienced sea lions nervously crane their necks looking out for orcas, the tall black fins slicing through the waves mean nothing to the innocent youngsters. In a single swift ambush, the enormous predators sail in on a wave, snatch a little pup, and carry it away between their teeth. Females heading toward or returning from their feeding trips are also taken, but the clumsy, bite-sized pups are an easier, if not tastier, meal. One in five sea lion mothers will lose her offspring to an orca by the end of the season.

The agile sea lions are able to reach speeds exceeding fifteen miles (24 km) per hour, but they can not outswim a hungry orca. It is estimated that every year some 500 of the peninsula's 19,000 sea lions succumb to these amazing predators, many of them in the shallows or even on the beach.

Reckless Taunting

A few seasons ago, a group of playful subadult sea lions tested their prowess by teasing the orcas. In a game of "catch-me-if-you-can," the swift sea lions swirled around the killer whales in tight circles, and crisscrossed just in front of their noses. But one day, they pushed the game too far: a visibly annoyed orca snapped up one of the pestering sea lions and, with the catch in its mouth, swam across the length of the rookery until every other sea lion had scrambled up the beach in terror.

Left: THE TIDES AT THE VALDÉS PENINSULA RISE AND FALL BY AS MUCH AS THIRTY-THREE FEET (10 M), AND ARE SAID TO BE SECOND IN THE WORLD ONLY TO THOSE OF CANADA'S BAY OF FUNDY. MANY OF THE SEA LION'S FAVORITE ROCKS ARE HIGH AND DRY WHEN THE TIDE GOES DOWN. IF THE SEA LIONS DO NOT DESCEND IN TIME TO REACH THE WATER, THEY MAY HAVE TO JUMP FROM WHAT SOON BECOMES A STEEP CLIFF, OR WAIT FOR MANY HOURS IN BLISTERING SUMMER TEMPERATURES, UNTIL THE SEA RISES AGAIN. BY THE SAME TOKEN, THOSE ANIMALS IN THE WATER MAY FIND IT IMPOSSIBLE TO JOIN THEIR FRIENDS ON THE ROCKS.

Opposite: SEA LIONS HAVE BEEN OBSERVED TO EMIT STREAMS OF UNDERWATER CLICKS IN CONDITIONS OF POOR VISIBILITY. SOME SCIENTISTS BELIEVE THAT, LIKE DOLPHINS, THEY MAY BE ABLE TO ECHOLOCATE, BUT SO FAR THE EVIDENCE REMAINS INCONCLUSIVE.

Sea Lion Encounter

As I paddled back to the boat I found the little fair sea lion chewing at the anchor line. Like a dog with a toy he pulled it back and forth. He looked at me and curled backward, spiralling through the sea in long perfect loops. Then he paused. Floating in mid-water, he folded his foreflippers as if in contemplative prayer. Finally, he stretched them out to the side like the wings of a plane, and sailed through the glassy sea as if he were flying.

I dove under him and lay flat on the sand, looking up from below. Shafts of sunlight danced all around him, outlining his black silhouette against the cobalt blue sky. Slowly he spiralled down to me, inching closer and closer until his whiskers almost touched my mask, and stared at me intently. The sun reflected from his big, dark eyes, which to my surprise sparkled back in the most beautiful chestnut tones. He was so close that I could see his black pupils expand and contract as he focused on my face. God knows what was going through his mind.

In a sea of silence and light, time stood still as we eyed each other with mutual fascination. There was a sweetness and puppy-like innocence in his look that is still hard to describe. The urge to reach out and touch overwhelmed me and I slowly lifted my hand. For a moment I felt his soft, furry belly. Then he stiffened and shot away with barely a stroke of his paddle-shaped flippers. As he disappeared into the deep flurry of green, bubbles followed him like the tail of a comet.

Dusky Dolphin (LAGENORHYNCHUS OBSCURUS)

An Unexpected Rescue

On an early summer day in 1991, three fishermen were returning to camp with their harvest of scallops. When they crossed the Gulf of San José, their attention was caught by the frenzied splashes of the largest group of dolphins they had ever seen. In an exuberant display of joy, the entire school was somersaulting, spinning, and whirling, with dolphins soaring through the sky in spectacular leaps up to thirteen feet (4 m) high. Drawing closer, the men discovered that the commotion seemed to center around a particular group of dolphins that was milling about in their midst. Intrigued, two of the men got into the water.

The underwater cacophony of squeaks and whistles was overwhelming, and dolphins shot past them from all directions. Some two dozen dusky dolphins whirled around a single female, hovering at the water's surface. Just below her was the tiniest calf the fishermen had ever seen. A perfect replica of its mother, it was black on its topside, and shiny white underneath.

Dolphins are known to act as midwives to each other, assisting mother and calf through the difficult paces of birth. However, this calf floated motionless in mid-water, oblivious to the turmoil around it. Helpless and forlorn, it did not seeem to know how to breathe. Fearing for the calf's life, the fishermen swam over to help it. Suddenly, three large female sea lions emerged from below, gliding past them toward the lilliputian dolphin. Circling, they nuzzled and poked the tiny fellow with their snouts, gently nudging it toward the surface. With a delicate spew it took its first breath of air, flicked its minuscule tail, and huddled next to its exhausted mother's side.

The fishermen were exhilarated, but perplexed. The sea lions, which could have easily devoured the helpless calf, appeared to have come to its rescue. Was this empathy, motherly instinct, play, or yet another of the many secrets of the animal world?

Dusky dolphins are found exclusively in the southern hemisphere, where they inhabit the cool circumpolar waters of the southern latitudes, between thirty and fifty-eight degrees. They appear in three main, geographically isolated, populations: around New Zealand and southern Australia, off South Africa in the southern Indian Ocean, and clockwise around the coasts of South America.

In 1832 Charles Darwin first discovered the secluded population in the Gulf of San José. His HMS *Beagle* captured a dusky dolphin, which was named *Delphinus fitzroyi*, after the *Beagle's* captain Robert Fitzroy. The duskies seem to prefer the smaller gulf, where they can habitually be found from spring to early autumn. During the colder months of the year they migrate to more abundant feeding grounds, although some seem to remain year round.

Often described as capricious and moody, duskies seem to follow a somewhat rigid routine that appears to guide their behavioral patterns throughout the day: after spending their nights in the safety of shallow coastal waters far from menacing orcas and deep-water sharks, they begin their mornings in search of breakfast. Traveling in small groups, the dolphins swim about ten feet abreast of each other as they scan the area for prey with their ultrasonic clicks. They feed on a varied diet of mackerel, capelin, hake, squid, crustaceans, and anchovies, the latter being their favorite quarry during the summer months at Valdés.

The anchovy forays of duskies are reminiscent of the strategies the Norwegian orcas use to herd their herring. When they find a school of fish, they drive them against the surface by swimming around and beneath them in ever-tightening loops, while bombarding the fish with loud sounds to startle and stun them. One at a time, the dolphins break their formation to dash into the swirling mass of anchovies, filling their mouths during their lunges.

Duskies have a varied repertoire of leaps. Some are believed to serve specific purposes, such as enabling them to scan the horizon for feeding seabirds whose presence indicates a school of fish beneath the water's surface. Other times they will breach noisily around the periphery of a school of anchovies, landing particularly loudly on their side or back to drive the terrified fish into a tight cluster. This also helps the dusky to announce its position to other dolphins in the area.

The sound created by the duskies' breaches reverberates through the underwater world. Their splashes can be seen for miles, attracting large clouds of birds and even more dolphins to the scene. The arrival of other members increases the success of herding the great swarm of fish. As they all cooperate, each dolphin gets its share of the catch.

Up to three hundred duskies congregate on such days and feeding may continue for hours, accompanied by much socializing and play. The excitement is contagious and the pace picks up toward the end of the feast as more and more dolphins, their stomachs full, begin to frolic. Duskies are veritable acrobats, and they will somersault, backflip, and spin around in mid-air with stunning grace, thrashing the sea white with the splashes of the entire school.

In summer, when anchovies abound, the duskies look for food during the day, then rest at night. In winter their routine is reversed, and they rest during the day and forage at night, presumably on bottom-dwelling fish. However, even during the summer months, the dolphins do not always find anchovies. On such days, they remain in small foraging groups and socialize little during their quest for food.

Dusky dolphins live in open societies. Members come and go among various groups, the size and composition of which change dramatically according to the activity the dolphins are pursuing. At Valdés, the ideal foraging group for duskies seems to consist of six to fifteen dolphins. Only in the months of

plenty do they gather in large active groups for a big feast. A couple of hours afterward, they splinter back into smaller subgroups.

Although duskies have a more fluid social system than the permanent orca pods, for example, steady relationships, such as long-term associations between mothers and their offspring and other, probably related, individuals, do exist in dusky society. Two duskies that were tagged off Valdés were found still together seven years later.

Trying to attract the attention of a group of duskies during their matinal forays is practically impossible since they go about their tasks with impervious stubbornness. Once they have eaten their fill, however, they become jovial and friendly. In the afternoons, the disinterested foraging groups of the morning suddenly become approachable and highly curious, playing with any animal or object that crosses their path. They cavort with sea lions and swirl around right whales, occasionally hitching a ride on the big whale's pressure wave by swimming just ahead of it. When humans approach, the duskies are inquisitive, sprinting over to bowride on a boat or investigate divers in the water.

Seaweed Games

I spent nearly two weeks trying to photograph duskies underwater. But whenever I plunged into the icy swells, they would charge toward me, only to torpedo straight past, disappearing into the cloudy green soup ahead. Undoubtedly, they had inspected me, although I had barely seen them.

On the last day, I spotted a group of about a dozen duskies. The polished surface of the sea glowed like an emerald in the afternoon sun, and for once it was not so bitterly cold. As soon as they saw the skiff, the duskies came racing over, riding in our wake until the boat came to a halt and I jumped into the water.

Circling around me, they chirped and squeaked, swimming sideways to catch a better glimpse (since their eyes are located on the sides of their head). They seemed to be everywhere at once—below, behind, ahead, above. I turned and turned, trying to follow their movements.

Suddenly, one dolphin swam toward me with a piece of seaweed in its beak. Stopping just a foot away from me, he let it go, nudging it gently toward my face. When I did not react, he snapped it up again and sped away. A few moments later the dolphin returned. This time the weed was draped neatly over its left flipper, like some peculiar scarf. He let it go in front of me. Finally, I understood, and tossed it out of the water as far as I could. Like a dog retrieving a stick, he picked it up and promptly brought it back, and I threw it again.

A couple of minutes into the game, a smaller dolphin edged toward me, looking as if he was having enormous trouble swimming . No wonder! A giant clump of seaweed was draped over the base of his tail! How am I ever supposed to throw that for him? I wondered, regretting that I could not reward him for his huge efforts!

Dusky dolphins in New Zealand regularly engage in this form of aquatic handball, meticulously passing the algae from one swimmer to the next. When a group of researchers tried to entice bottlenose dolphins in the Bahamas to play the same game, they willingly accepted the gift and sped away with it. For now, this appears to be a game played exclusively by the duskies.

Page 123: DUSKIES ARE THE MOST COMMON SPECIES OF DOLPHIN AT VALDÉS. THEY ARE MORE PETITE THAN BOTTLENOSE DOLPHINS, THEIR COMPACT BODIES RARELY EXCEEDING SIX FEET (2 M) IN LENGTH. UNLIKE THEIR LARGER COUSINS' PROMINENT BEAK, THEY HAVE A SHORT AND STUBBY BLACK SNOUT. UNLIKE ORCAS AND BOTTLENOSE DOLPHINS, DUSKIES ADAPT POORLY TO CAPTIVITY, WHERE THEY TEND TO DIE QUICKLY. TODAY THEY ARE FOUND ONLY IN THE WILD.

Right: LIKE ORCAS, DUSKIES ARE COATED IN STRIKING PATTERNS OF PIGMENTATION, THE CONTRAST OF COLORS DIFFUSING AND BLURRING THEIR NATURAL SHAPE SO AS TO DECEIVE THEIR PREY. AS WITH ORCAS, THEIR DARK GRAY BACKS AND SNOWY UNDERSIDES PROVIDE A FORM OF COUNTERSHADING. THEIR FACES ARE WHITE, EXCEPT FOR THE FAINT HINT OF A BLACK BEAK AND A SMALL SOMBER SPECTACLE AROUND THEIR EYES. THEIR FLIPPERS ARE GRAY, AND THEY HAVE A TALL CONCAVE DORSAL FIN THAT IS LIGHTER TOWARD THE REAR. FROM BELOW AND BEHIND THEIR DORSAL FIN DOWN TO THEIR RAVEN TAILS, A PALER FORKED STREAK CUTS LIKE A PAIR OF SUSPENDERS ACROSS THEIR SILVERY FLANKS.

Bottlenose Dolphin (TURSIOPS TRUNCATUS)

Bottlenose dolphins are probably the best-known marine mammal in the world. Protagonists of the famous "Flipper" television series, they grace most dolphin shows in marine parks. Their appearance in a wide range of coastal habitats, such as bays and estuaries, lower ranges of rivers, and even harbors, makes them one of the most commonly sighted species. Avid bowriders, they are friendly and curious, and in some areas actively seek out human contact. In some parts of the world they even cooperate with local fishermen, driving fish into their nets, for which they receive a share of the catch.

Bottlenose dolphins may grow to almost thirteen feet (4 m) in length, but their shape, size, and coloration vary tremendously in different regions of the world, a sign of their supreme adaptation to a wide range of environmental conditions. Attempts to categorize bottlenose dolphins into twelve different species (*Tursiops gephyreus* for the South Atlantic population), have met with dispute in the scientific community, and so far only two different ecotypes are commonly recognized: a larger offshore and a smaller inshore population.

Unlike orcas and dusky dolphins, the body of the bottlenose dolphin is covered in a nondescript cape of uniform color, which varies from a subdued blend of brown to different shades of gray. This coloring fades out toward the flanks, exposing a milky white or pinkish belly. While the bottlenose dolphins of northern Argentina are silvery gray and have a rather triangular dorsal fin, the population at Valdés is charcoal with a notably concave dorsal fin.

There are some striking similarities between orcas and bottlenose dolphins: bottlenose dolphins are truly cosmopolitan, inhabiting almost all of the world's oceans. Unlike their larger relatives, they prefer tropical and temperate seas, and do not appear in the icy waters of the polar regions. Their diet is varied, according to local conditions. Their hunting methods are also highly adaptive, and are often based on cooperative strategies.

THE BOTTLENOSE DOLPHIN'S MOST PROMINENT FEATURE IS ITS TRADEMARK CYLINDRICAL BEAK, AFTER WHICH IT HAS BEEN NAMED.

Some of their more spectacular feeding techniques include chasing fish onto mud flats, temporarily beaching themselves before they wiggle back out to sea, and stunning or killing fish by smacking them with their tails and sending them flying through the air. Like orcas, they sometimes play with their catch.

At the Valdés Peninsula, they are presumed to feed on false sea salmon, southern anchovies, hake, pollock, and squid. They usually appear in small groups and can be observed swimming in the surf or riding breaking rollers close to shore.

Sea lions are welcome playmates, and they occasionally swim alongside right whales. For no apparent reason however, their relationship with their smaller cousin, the dusky dolphin, is one of mutual indifference. Their amazing ability to adapt to varying habitats allows them to migrate to different geographical areas in response to climactic and environmental fluctuations and temporary food shortages.

Unfortunately, there has been a marked decline in the number of bottlenose sightings at the Valdés Peninsula over the last two decades. Sightings have become more sporadic and the dolphins appear in smaller numbers. For reasons we do not yet understand, they may have permanently settled in a more favorable territory.

Chapter Two
Birds of Coastal Patagonia

Patagonia's shoreline is bathed by the Malvinas current, whose cold Antarctic waters, rich in plankton and nutrients, support a vast food chain, from the tiniest invertebrates to large schools of fishes, marine mammals, and seabirds.

From their breeding grounds on the Malvinas Islands, black-browed albatrosses (*Diomedea melanophrys*) follow the rich Malvinas current northward, snatching their favorite quarry, Patagonian *lolligo* and short-finned *illex* squid, right off the surface. This is how they come to appear along the shores of the Valdés Peninsula, where they feed on swarms of

anchovies alongside another imposing denizen of the circumpolar regions, the southern giant petrel (*Macronectes giganteus*).

Rock cormorants (*Phalacrocorax magellanicus*), which are confined to southern South America, nest precariously along the peninsula's steep, yellow cliffs, and alongside olivaceous cormorants (*Phalacrocorax olivaceus*), at Isla de los Pájaros, a five-acre (2.2-ha) island, just a half mile (800 m) offshore, at the southern tip of the Gulf of San José.

The blue-eyed king cormorant (*Phalacrocorax albiventer*) breeds colonially on relatively flat territory, such as low sea cliffs and promontories, both on the peninsula and at Punta Tombo. A fourth cormorant species, the guanay (*Phalacrocorax bougainvillii*), was thought to be confined to the coasts of Chile and Peru until it was found nesting at Punta Tombo among king and rock cormorants, making Punta Tombo one of the few nesting sites in the world for three cormorant species. Sadly, the rookery, which lies at the very tip of the Tombo headland, has been washed away by periodic summer storms and has also been damaged by many years of uncontrolled access by tourists. Over two decades, the number of cormorants nesting at Punta Tombo has fallen from an estimated 8,000 birds in 1964 to barely 500 birds in 1997. The guanay cormorant continues to be exceptionally rare in the province of Chubut.

The Valdés Peninsula and Punta Tombo are also home to three species of oystercatcher: the Magellanic oystercatcher (*Haematopus leucopodus*), with its golden eyes with a deep yellow ring; the American oystercatcher (*Haematopus palliatus*), which has yellow-orange eyes with a distinctive red eye ring and darker red beak; and the larger, blackish oystercatcher (*Haematopus ater*), which is entirely black and has yellow-orange eyes with a red rim. The blackish oystercatcher travels in pairs or in small groups of up to six birds and feeds almost exclusively on hard-shelled mollusks in rocky, intertidal areas. It is less agressive and noisy than the other two species, which have a continuous, piercing call, and is the only oystercatcher that stays at the Valdés Peninsula year-round.

Punta Tombo is the largest continental penguin rookery in the world, with over half a million Magellanic penguins (*Spheniscus magellanicus*). Other nesting birds include Antarctic skuas (*Catharacta antarctica*), kelp or dominican gulls (*Larus dominicanus*), and dolphin gulls (*Larus [Leucophaeus] scoresbii*). In 1997, the total population of dolphin gulls in Argentine Patagonia was estimated at only 700 pairs in twenty-six colonies. Dolphin gulls tend to nest in small colonies of sixteen to twenty-four pairs, and lay two eggs which are incubated between twenty-four and twenty-seven days. Chicks hatch between mid- and late December, but over 40 percent of the eggs are lost to predators, and even in the most successful years, less than half of the dolphin gull chicks survive their first three weeks of life.

Left: THE SMALL, DOVE-GRAY DOLPHIN GULL INHABITS SOUTHERN SOUTH AMERICA, INCLUDING TIERRA DEL FUEGO. THE VALDÉS PENINSULA LIES AT THE NORTHERNMOST BOUNDARY OF ITS RANGE. IT NESTS AT PUNTA TOMBO, WHERE IT SCOURS FOR SCRAPS OF REGURGITATED FOOD FROM THE CORMORANT AND PENGUIN COLONY AND BOLDLY RAIDS THE NESTS OF CORMORANTS AND THE CONSIDERABLY LARGER KELP GULLS TO FEED ON THEIR EGGS. DOLPHIN GULLS ALSO FEED ON MOLLUSKS AND OTHER INVERTEBRATES IN THE INTERTIDAL ZONE, BUT THEY ARE PRIMARILY SCAVENGERS. THEY COME TO PUNTA TOMBO BETWEEN SEPTEMBER AND FEBRUARY, WHEN FOOD FROM BREEDING PENGUIN, CORMORANT, AND KELP GULL COLONIES IS MOST ABUNDANT.

Opposite: THE KELP GULL INHABITS THE CIRCUMPOLAR REGIONS OF THE SOUTHERN HEMISPHERE, AND CAN BE FOUND FROM SOUTHERN BRAZIL TO TIERRA DEL FUEGO, AND FROM SOUTH AFRICA TO SOUTHERN AUSTRALIA AND NEW ZEALAND. ALTHOUGH THERE ARE OVER FORTY SPECIES OF GULLS IN THE WORLD, THE KELP GULL IS THE ONLY ONE THAT BREEDS ON SUB-ANTARCTIC ISLANDS AND ON THE ANTARCTIC CONTINENT AS FAR AS SIXTY-EIGHT DEGREES SOUTH LATITUDE.

The kelp gull feeds on mollusks and invertebrates in intertidal zones, such as the mussel beds that remain exposed during low tide along the peninsula's long reefs. At the Punta Tombo penguin colony, however, kelp gulls scour for abandoned eggs and spilled regurgitated food left over from adults feeding their chicks, and terrorize penguin parents with their habit of attacking unprotected chicks. In recent years they have also developed a taste for whale skin and blubber, which they gouge right off the whale's backs. The smallest of the peninsula's gulls, the brown-hooded gull *(Larus maculipennis),* has also caught on to this menacing habit, which has escalated to a severe degree of harassment of the whales.

Another fierce aerial pirate is the Antarctic skua, which will readily attack cormorants and terns in mid-air, pulling at their wings or tails until they drop or regurgitate their catch. At Punta Tombo, Antarctic skuas prey on penguin and cormorant eggs; small and weak chicks; and, to a lesser extent, on weakened adults and carcasses. They also feed on shrimp, but like the kelp gulls, they prefer to obtain their shrimp second-hand, in the form of spilled regurgitated food left by adult penguins feeding their chicks. Smaller than adult penguins, skuas depend on stealth and speedy surprise attacks. They are very efficient predators that often work in pairs to distract an adult penguin and steal its eggs or chicks, or to attack gulls and snatch their quarry.

Like skuas and kelp gulls, the snowy sheathbill *(Chionis alba)* relishes regurgitated shrimp, krill, and fish that drop to the ground as penguins and cormorants feed their chicks, and they will not shy away from stealing eggs or taking the occasional small, live chick. It is known as the southern hemisphere's garbage collector. Like a domestic chicken, this stocky, pigeon-like bird struts between ranks of pen-

Opposite: THE SANDERLING (CALIDRIS ALBA) *BREEDS ON THE NORTH AMERICAN TUNDRA, BUT WINTERS ALONG THE PATAGONIAN COAST. BETWEEN SEPTEMBER AND APRIL, FLOCKS OF FIFTY TO SEVERAL HUNDRED BIRDS CAN BE SEEN FEEDING ON TINY CRUSTACEANS AND MOLLUSKS ALONG THE PENINSULA'S REEFS DURING LOW TIDE. THESE LITTLE SHOREBIRDS FLY IN SUCH TIGHT FORMATION THAT CLOUDS OF SANDERLINGS SWOOSH ALONG THE SHORE-LINE, TURNING HERE AND THERE AS IF A SINGLE ORGANISM.*

Below: THE SNOWY SHEATHBILL DERIVES ITS NAME FROM ITS SNOW-WHITE PLUMAGE AND HORNY SHEATH THAT COVERS ITS NOS-TRILS AND GROWS OVER PART OF ITS BILL. IT BREEDS ON SUB-ANTARCTIC ISLANDS AND IN THE ANTARCTIC PENINSULA AS FAR AS SIXTY-FIVE DEGREES SOUTH.*

guins, sea lions, and elephant seals, pecking at any-thing remotely resembling food. The sheathbill is an opportunistic scavenger that adapts easily to its sea-sonally changing prey. During the sea lion and ele-phant seal breeding seasons, afterbirths and pup carcasses constitute the mainstay of its diet, although it also feeds on milk from nursing cows and on feces. The snowy sheathbill is a bit of an enigma to taxono-mists. It belongs to none of the traditional seabird families and seems to fall between shorebirds (waders) and gulls and skuas (jaegers).

Above: AT PUNTA TOMBO, THE ANTARCTIC SKUA BREEDS IN LATE SPRING AND EARLY SUMMER, WHEN FOOD FROM THE NEIGH-BORING PENGUIN COLONY IS MOST READILY AVAILABLE. THEIR NESTS ARE SIMPLE SCRAPES IN THE GROUND, WITHOUT MUCH ADDED MATERIAL, AND ARE CONSPICU-OUSLY SPACED APART TO REDUCE CANNI-BALISM BY HUNGRY NEIGHBORS.*

Magellanic Penguin (SPHENISCUS MAGELLANICUS)

The Magellanic penguin was named after Ferdinand Magellan, the explorer whose 1519 expedition first came upon these birds. When Magellan entered the strait that today bears his name, he reported seeing a large number of geese: "These geese are black and have all their feathers alike, both on body and wings. They do not fly and live on fish." In just a short time he loaded his five ships with these peculiar "geese" to provision his sailors; in just one day, Sir Francis Drake's sailors killed three thousand penguins for food. Their flesh, he wrote, was "not unlike fat goose in England."

Apart from being a tasty meal, however, the charm of the little birds in their black tuxedos that walk upright like human beings, eluded the early explorers. Herman Melville, in his 1856 account of his trip around Cape Horn, described the penguins as ghastly creatures:

> Their bodies are grotesquely misshapen; their bills short, their feet seemingly legless, while the members at their sides are neither fin, wings, nor arm. And truly neither fish, flesh nor fowl, is the penguin; . . . without exception the most ambiguous and least lovely creature yet discovered by man. Though dabbling in all three elements, and indeed possessing some rudimental claims to all, the penguin is at home in none. On land it stumps; afloat it sculls; in the air it flops.

He was right on two accounts, for penguins are rather ungainly on land, and despite being birds, do not fly—at least not in the air. They are truly extraordinary however, in their adaptation to life in the sea. Endowed with special filtering glands, penguins are able to drink seawater, ejecting excess salt through their nostrils. Aerial birds have long, thin feathers, large wings, and hollow bones for lightness in the air. Penguins on the other hand, are the most marine adapted of all birds, with heavy bones to swim underwater, and short, scale-like feathers that lie close to the body and which are tightly packed to keep them dry at sea.

In the ocean, penguins, so hefty on land, are suddenly weightless. With powerful, downward thrusts of

their short, paddle-like wings, penguins can gracefully "fly" through the water as smoothly as other birds do in the air. Their stubby tails and broad, wedge-shaped feet serve as rudders. The Magellanic penguin usually travels at speeds of about five miles (8 km) per hour. But, because they are shaped like tiny submarines, they can reach velocities of up to fifteen miles (24 km) per hour when pursuing fish or fleeing a predator. In order to breathe while traveling quickly they "porpoise," just like dolphins and sea lions, leaping clear of the water.

The Colonies at Punta Tombo and the Valdés Peninsula

The Magellanic penguin's rookeries vary widely in size, and can be found in a variety of habitats, including banks, sandy hills, grassy slopes, woodlands, and even occasionally on tiers of cliff faces. In order to seek protection from the scorching summer sun and from predators, most Magellanic penguins dig shallow burrows into soft soil or nest in the shadow of bushes.

EVERY YEAR, IN THE FINAL DAYS OF THE AUSTRAL WINTER, THE FIRST PENGUIN MALES, PLUMP FROM MONTHS OF FISHING AT SEA, WADDLE ONTO THE BEACHES AT PUNTA TOMBO AND CALETA VALDÉS AND MAKE THEIR WAY TO THEIR TRADITIONAL BURROWS.

Punta Tombo is home to the largest continental penguin colony in the world, with over half a million Magellanic penguins coming to its shores every year. Some 250,000 pairs nest over an area of about a square mile (2.5 sq. km).

In the late 1960s small numbers of penguins also began to breed at the Valdés Peninsula, which is thought to be their northernmost breeding ground. The peninsula's colonies are expanding rapidly. In just one decade, the small colony at Estancia San Lorenzo ballooned from 93 nests in 1977 to an estimated 18,000 nests in 1993. And while in 1989 only seven penguin pairs bred next to ten other bird species at Isla de Los Pájaros, 47 couples nested on the island in 1994. By the mid-1990s an estimated 45,000 Magellanic penguins bred on the peninsula, most of them on the islands and shores of Caleta Valdés. The growth of the Valdés colony is probably due to an influx of young birds from other, more traditional, rookeries to the south, such as Punta Tombo, Punta Clara, and Cabo Dos Bahías. Why they moved to the Valdés Peninsula is anyone's guess.

Penguin Seasons and Cycles

Year after year, the Magellanic penguin's cycle of life follows the seasons. Spring and summer are spent on land, autumn and winter at sea.

The Magellanic penguin migrates from its northern wintering grounds to its southern ancestral breeding areas along Patagonia's shore. Like elephant seals, penguins have a terrestrial and a pelagic phase, with a remarkable ability to conquer both land and sea. Although they spend most of their life in the water, penguins are birds, after all, and must return to land for two reasons: to lay eggs and to grow new feathers.

During the annual molting period, which lasts two to three weeks, the penguins need extra reserves of fat to grow new feathers while fasting on land. During this time, their coats temporarily lose their impermeability, making it impossible for them to feed at sea. Like elephant seals, adult penguins consume extra amounts of food to gain weight prior to molting. But many juvenile penguins, which were not fat enough when they first arrived, cannot survive their forced stay on land, and starve to death.

Magellanic penguins have a strong sense of fidelity to their traditional breeding areas and even to the same burrow, which they use year after year. In late August, the first penguin males waddle onto the same shore they left almost half a year earlier and make their way inland to last year's burrow. Before the females arrive, the males clean out the nest and line it with grasses, twigs, and other suitable materials.

The Home Burrow

The penguin males guard their burrows with vigor, and usurpers are kicked out unceremoniously. For those that are still single, a nest well shaded under a bush or a spacious subterranean burrow not too far from the sea is the best guarantee to find a mate. To attract a female, penguin males puff up their chests, stretch out their wings and necks, and bray as loudly as they can. During braying contests, clusters of males carefully space their calls so as to not coincide with each other. Each male has a slightly different bray, which a female can distinguish among thousands. At Punta Tombo, where tens of thousands of braying penguins advertise empty nests, warn off competitors, and call to returning mates, the continuous cacophony is overpowering.

Some 80 percent of the male penguins and 70 percent of the females return to the same nest from

one season to the next, and some sites are used by a couple over many consecutive years. As they wander through a colony, sheep, guanacos, and rheas occasionally step onto a burrow and break into it. Burrows may be washed away during flash floods. Bushes may be eaten by sheep or die when the relentless Patagonian wind uproots them from the sandy soil. Such nest sites offer only scant shelter at best, but the penguins' instincts are stronger than circumstance.

To find out what occurs when the penguins are no longer able to physically access their habitual nests, Dee Boersma, who has been studying the Punta Tombo colony since 1982, temporarily locked several birds out of their old nests. Before they laid their eggs, she fenced off bushes and filled burrows with rocks. But the penguins were not interested in finding a new nest. They waddled around the barriers, trying to find

a weakness in the structures, or to dig tunnels underneath the enclosures. Most eventually settled nearby. But one particular bird, which had nested under a bush, managed to climb up a fence placed over it and get inside. It appeared perfectly content to be trapped inside the enclosure, as long as it was at home.

Penguin Romance

By mid-September, the onset of the austral spring, the first tubby females arrive on the shores. Like the males, they have navigated unerringly across vast tracts of ocean, some traveling 2,000 miles (3,000 km) from the north, off the coast of Brazil. By the end of the month, the trickle of penguins has turned into a flood. Like waiters in a flurry, long lines of black and white birds stream along traditional paths. In some areas, hundreds of penguins waddle along like

humans on a busy street during rush hour.

The arriving females waste no time and march straight up the slopes to their nests. When, after many months at sea, a female returns to her nest and mate, the reunion is enthusiastic. Elaborate greeting ceremonies reaffirm old bonds, while ensuing courtship rituals release hormones that stimulate synchronized breeding in both partners. In their first days together, the pair copulates several times, to ensure that the female conceives. Single females wander from contender to contender, who all bray for their attention. When a female finally chooses a mate, she signals her approval by entering her new residence— a generous word for a shriveled bush or a dusty hole in the ground.

Penguin Reunions

One clear, cool morning in early September, I visited a small penguin colony along the banks of Caleta Valdés, where the first male birds had gathered on the pebbled beach. Some clustered together to "bill duel," which biologists believe decides social rank. Others bathed in the shallows, swaying gently from side to side in the morning swells.

The sandstone cliff was punctured with round, dusty hollows, the empty residences from last year's breeding season. I sat down on a small, flat ledge that protruded from the cliff. Strange rasping and scratching sounds emanated from somewhere above me along the sandy walls.

Suddenly, a shower of sand and pebbles landed right on my head. I looked up and found myself staring straight at the short, brush-like tail of a penguin that was anchored into the sandy wall with the claws of one webbed foot and was furiously scraping away with the other. Again he sent down a cascade of dirt and rocks. This time I ducked, though my jerky response alerted

him of my presence. He turned, and stared down at me. He was round and fat and wore a smattering of big black polka dots atop his snowy chest. As we gazed at each other, he began to swing his head from side to side. I too, swung my head from side to side, and as if playing a game, the penguin mimicked my movements. Later I found out that this had not been a form of play, but a sign of defense and alarm, and I regretted having frightened him.

When I returned the following week, the scene had changed dramatically. Many birds had left the beach and had moved up the slope. At the bottom of the hill, a handful of penguins stood proud and straight next to low, spiky bushes like an assembly of liveried butlers. Others rested at the entrance of low, dusty burrows, while some could be heard still excavating inside their dwellings. A few were shuffling about carrying pieces of grass, gull feathers, twigs, and in one case, an old cigarette pack, to line their nests. Where the sandstone was steep, the penguins leaned forward and hopped up the cliff side like puppets on short, bouncy springs.

Everyone was getting ready for the arrival of the females. A raucous serenade of staccato braying echoed through the colony: the males were all trilling at the top of their lungs, including my polka-dotted friend.

I decided to name him José, and returned daily to watch his progress. Soon he got used to my presence and completely ignored me. Thanks to his unusual spots, José was easy to recognize, even from afar—provided he faced my way.

One day I noticed another penguin hopping across the ledge toward José's home. A female, I thought, delighted at the prospect. But I was wrong. José shot out of the burrow and attacked the visitor with such viciousness and determination that both birds slipped and rolled down the hill where they fluttered across the ground, pecking at each other furiously. One of them fell into the entrance of a subterranean burrow, the other plunging behind, delivering nasty stabs to the head and chest. Finally the intruder stumbled away, while an exhausted José stood panting at the bottom of the hill. When evening fell I found him lying outside his cave, his chest encrusted with blood. He had bravely defended all that mattered: a home for a future generation. Hopefully, he would soon find the companion he deserved.

By the end of the month, two penguins peeked out of most burrows, and from underneath most bushes. But José remained single. Whenever I came to visit him he stood like a sentinel in front of his empty nest, his lonely brays reverberating through the colony, announcing his unhappy state. He had worked hard to improve the burrow, but so far no female seemed to want to settle in with him. Was it because he lived too far up the hill, a considerable hike from the sea?

The egg-laying season would soon begin, and José's chances of attracting a mate were dwindling with every passing day. Then to my great surprise, several days after the fight, I found José with another penguin. Holding his bill to his chest, he walked around her with great pride, taking small deliberate steps on his short, stubby legs. Soon the female began circling around José until they

danced around each other in loops. After a while, José let out a loud, triumphant bray, waddled over, and began gently to preen her feathers.

I couldn't believe my eyes. They stood together like bosom friends that had never been apart, and I wondered whether she was his lifetime partner who had become delayed on her journey to Valdés, or whether he had managed to attract a new female. After a while, the female turned around, ducked, and disappeared inside the burrow. This was a sign that she had accepted José as her mate, and I decided to call her María.

José and María spent much of the following days lovingly preening each other, and occasionally waddling down to the beach to collect algae for their nest. One sunny morning I found José excitedly tapping his bill against María's, while patting her frantically with his tapered flippers. María lay down, and allowed José to gently peck at her back and neck with a passion unimaginable for such gawky creatures. When he finally mounted her I was certain their hard-earned union would end in success.

Occasionally a mated female penguin arrives a little late in the season and finds her partner has already invited another female into their home. The adulterous female is usually kicked out of the nest immediately by means of a nasty fight and the original couple settles back in together as if nothing ever happened.

Still, despite their tendency toward possessive behavior, almost a quarter of the penguins switch to a new partner after a period of five years.

The Next Generation

Once they have settled with a partner, the mated penguin pair remains together until the female lays the first creamy white egg. Having fasted for at least two weeks, while reconstructing his burrow and fighting off other males, the exhausted male finally abandons the nest to forage at sea. Egg-laying begins in the first days of October and continues throughout the month. The first chicks hatch in the second week of November, after forty to forty-two days of incubation. The female stays behind incubating the egg, and lays a second egg four days later. After three weeks the male returns, and takes over the incubation duty, while his starving mate embarks on a two-week fishing trip. Upon her return she warms the clutch for another week, while the male goes out again. A few days later, he comes home with a crop full of food, just in time to watch the first chick hatch, and he offers it a first meal of regurgitated fish porridge.

During the last week of incubation, many penguin parents alternate nesting duties every other day to ensure that when the time comes, one parent is present with food to feed the hatchlings. Once the chicks are hatched, the parents face a difficult challenge: their hungry brood is in one world, their food in another. The whistling and begging of the insatiable chicks is constant. To satisfy their rapacious appetites, both parents alternate guarding and fishing duties every two days, bringing home enough food to feed both chicks once a day.

It may take a baby penguin over a day to break out of its shell. The tiny chick weighs about three and a half ounces (100 g). Its thin, silvery down does not suffice to keep it warm, and it must be brooded until it develops a fluffy, gray-brown coat. For the first three weeks of their lives the newly-hatched penguins are never left alone. But by late December most parents are regularly foraging at sea, returning only for brief feeding stints at the nest. By January, when the fluffy-gray chicks are about two months old and weigh a little over two pounds (about 1 kg) they may venture away from their burrow and join a chick in another nest.

Survival

Few penguin chicks manage to survive the first months of their life: just over half of the eggs laid actually hatch, and then over half of the chicks die before they can fledge.

Nothing is more important than the proper coordination of nesting and fishing duties between penguin parents, for if the couple fails to balance properly the timing of nest changeovers, it jeopardizes the survival of its brood. Magellanic penguins do not sacrifice themselves for the survival of their progeny, and a starving parent will abandon the nest if its partner does not return in time. Abandoned eggs are a delicacy for scavenging skuas, sheathbills, gulls, foxes and armadillos, some of which will also take small, live chicks when they are unprotected.

At Punta Tombo, skuas and the large number of kelp gulls are a constant source of terror. These scavengers and opportunists rely on the negligence of penguin parents to prey upon abandoned eggs and small chicks, which they can carry away with a single swoop from the sky. Gulls often skip through the colony looking for scraps, such as spilled regurgitated food and carrion, while avoiding the pecks of adult penguins.

Sibling Rivalry

María laid her first egg in the second week of October, although I was unable to see the egg underneath her. That was when José finally abandoned the nest. He had fasted for an exceptionally long time and needed to replenish his fat reserves. María spent the rest of the month alone, inside the nest, occasionally getting up to reposition her eggs. In the first week of November, José returned to take over the incubation duty. The greeting with María was ecstatic. Almost two weeks later, María came home for her shift at warming the eggs.

With the eggs about to hatch I visited the nest several times a day. By the third day, one egg had rolled to the edge of the nest and lay in front of María's head. It had a tiny crack. To my surprise I could hear a barely audible peep from inside the shell, and María responded by gently tapping it with her bill. By nightfall however, the crack had barely widened, and I went home anxious I was going to miss the most important moment of my penguin family's life.

When I returned at the crack of dawn, José and María were preening each other at the entrance of the nest. The egg was now half open, and a minute wet

chick was lying on the sandy floor, still crouched inside half of the shell. After a while María left for the water and José settled on top of the half-hatched chick. The next morning I heard a faint high-pitched whistle. Underneath José's right flipper was the tiniest chick I had ever seen. Its feathers had dried, and it was covered with sparse gray down, with pinkish skin shining through underneath.

Peeping desperately, the fuzzy chick emerged from under José's wing. Its eyes were partly closed and it could barely hold up its head. After a few minutes, José regurgitated a pinkish meal of fish and squid. But the inexperienced chick only became covered in the slimy porridge, most of which dropped to the floor of the burrow. Still peeping urgently, the little chick was finally rewarded with a second, slightly more successful feed, during which it literally disappeared inside its father's throat. I named it Uno, since it was the firstborn. María took over the nest that afternoon, but for the next two days I could not see the other egg, and had no clue whether it was hatching or had died.

On the fourth day, José got up, and little cheeping Uno scrambled out from underneath him. From the back of the burrow came a second, barely audible peep. His brother, whom I called Dos, had finally hatched. He appeared to be less than an hour old, because his feathers were still damp and sticky.

Whenever José or María returned from fishing at sea, they were assaulted by their hungry chicks. Peeping shrilly, Uno and Dos would probe their parent's face and beak with their bills until they finally obtained the regurgitated food. Although José and María worked in shifts to supply daily meals of seafood porridge, tiny Dos struggled to feed from the very beginning.

Like most firstborn chicks, Uno had an advantage.

Born four days earlier, he was lively and strong and had already opened his eyes by the time the miniature Dos finally broke the shell of his egg. At feeding time, Uno would boldly shove past Dos and lunge toward José's or María's bill, his little head disappearing inside his parent's throat, greedily gulping down as much food as he possibly could. If Dos managed to get to the parent first, Uno would bat him away with his little flippers or trample over him, and I once even found Uno feeding while standing on top of his little brother.

José and María would feed alternatively to either side, and occasionally Dos was in a favorable spot when feeding began. That would drive Uno crazy and he would try to slip underneath or clamber over the parent to intercept the meal. Yet that was not always easy, and on lucky days, Dos had some time to feed in peace, while a desperate Uno frantically scrambled about on the other side.

After a feed, Uno's belly would be so swollen that he would have to take a deep nap in the back of the burrow. Dos, on the other hand, rarely slept and was left cheeping for more sustenance, long after the parents had no more to give. He was small and thin, and by the time he was three weeks old, the pear-shaped, pot-bellied Uno had monopolized so much food that he appeared nearly twice as large.

One day I found Dos at a neighboring burrow. A penguin parent was in the process of feeding its hungry brood. Dos cleverly maneuvered himself between the two older chicks and managed to steal a few morsels from the parent's bill. When the penguin parent regurgitated again, the excitement was too much for little Dos and he began to cheep. Hearing the interloper's voice the penguin parent realized Dos did not belong, and thrusting forward, jabbed hard at Dos with its bill. Dos stumbled away, bleeding from his head. He never made it back to his family.

When hungry, they can turn into fearsome predators that will snatch live chicks right from the side of their parents, and occasionally even attack large chicks that have grown too big and heavy to be carried away. The gulls kill these larger chicks by jabbing at their heads, and then consume them on the spot.

Chick Abductions

Gulls often work in pairs and lure a parent away from the burrow. One day I observed such an attack on a penguin parent with a smallish gray chick. The burrow was on the outskirts of the colony under a low, shriveled bush that offered only scant protection.

A gull landed just in front of the nest, where it ran from side to side, probing the parent's reaction. Visibly annoyed, the penguin extended its flippers and leaned forward to peck at the intruder. But the swift gull easily evaded the penguin's clumsy advances. Soon a second gull landed in front of the penguin and began teasing it away from the bush.

All the while, the chick kept close to its parent. Suddenly one of the gulls jumped over to the back of the parent and began pulling at its tail. The penguin swiveled around with a raucous bray and tried to catch the pestering bird with its powerful beak. With the parent distracted, the second gull lunged at the helpless chick. Luckily, it was too heavy for the gull to fly away with, and its wild cheeps alerted the parent to its predicament, prompting it to scramble over and retrieve the chick just before the gull could drag it away.

The Magellanic penguin's habit of burrowing into the ground or under bushes does hamper the gull's ability to attack their guarded nests, which it is more prone to do with those penguin species that nest in the open. Chicks are therefore most at risk when they are still small but no longer brooded by their parents.

When they are about a month old, the chicks first begin peering out of the nest, and at about six weeks of age, they gradually venture outside to explore their surroundings. Starving chicks that stumble out of the burrow in search of food are quickly snatched up by these aerial predators.

Adult penguins are not threatened by gulls, but they do have to face a number of other predators. Giant petrels have been observed capturing and drowning healthy penguins at sea. Penguins are eaten by sharks and occasionally gulped down by a passing orca. Sea lion bulls capture Magellanic penguins, flicking them from side to side to separate the skin from the hide before they eat them. During the 1997 breeding season, a large bull elephant seal spent several weeks on a Punta Tombo beach, where he killed several dozen penguins—but such behavior is unusual.

A small number of penguins are hunted down while they are foraging for food, and never make it back to their brood. Those that return to the nest must do so in time. Hatchlings will quickly die of starvation, especially during their first week of life. Older chicks can wait, but only a few days.

First-born chicks are considerably more likely to survive than their siblings: by the time the second chick hatches the first born is much stronger and more aggressive. In years of plenty, both chicks usually make it through. Since the younger chick fledges later from the nest, it often manages to catch up in size and weight after its sibling has left. But when food is scarce, not enough is left over for the second chick after the first has eaten its fill, and sibling rivalry becomes an issue of life and death. In meager years, staggered hatching ensures that at least one chick—the older one—is well fed and has a chance to survive.

NEWBORN PENGUINS HAVE A SILVERY GRAY DOWN THAT SOON GROWS OUT UNTIL THEY ARE COVERED WITH A FLUFFY CLOVER-BROWN COAT. WHEN THEY ARE ABOUT FIVE WEEKS OLD, THE FIRST JUVENILE FEATHERS BEGIN TO PUSH OUT THE FLUFF. AS THE DOWN FALLS OUT, SMOOTH GRAYISH-WHITE COATS SHINE THROUGH UNDERNEATH. LIKE MOLTING ADULTS, THE CHICKS LOOK RAGGED AND TATTERED DURING THIS PROCESS, WITH PATCHES OF FURRY DOWN STICKING OUT ON THEIR BELLIES AND HEADS. WITHIN TWO MONTHS THEIR JUVENILE SUITS ARE GLISTENING AND COMPLETE. ALTHOUGH THEY ARE NOW READY TO ENTER THE WATER ON THEIR FIRST MIGRATION TO NORTHERN FEEDING GROUNDS, THEY MUST YET DEVELOP THE CHARACTERISTIC DOUBLE CHEST BANDS OF FULL-GROWN MAGELLANIC PENGUINS. NOT UNTIL THEY RETURN THE FOLLOWING SEASON WILL THEY EXCHANGE THEIR JUVENILE PLUMAGE FOR THE STARK, BLACK AND WHITE TUXEDO LOOK OF THE ADULT PENGUIN.

The higher a chick's body weight, the more likely it is to fledge. But even if a chick manages to fledge from the nest, it may not live through the molt in the following year to become an adult. Ironically, penguins often starve during the molt, even though they are right next to the sea, because they are unable to forage until they have grown their feathers. Even among those young penguins that do manage to fledge, almost 90 percent do not live through their first year at sea. Chicks must be in prime condition and need to learn quickly how to hunt for food in the sea if they are to survive.

Human Impact

Those penguins that make their way back to Punta Tombo the following season have overcome the worst. Once they molt out of their pale yearling suits into the ringed black and white adult frock, they can look forward to at least a decade of successful breeding, and some lucky ones may even live to a maximum lifespan, estimated between twenty-five and thirty years.

Although adult Magellanic penguins enjoy a healthy annual survival rate of about 90 percent, this no longer depends on successfully evading natural

Opposite: THE MOLTING SEASON BEGINS IN FEBRUARY, WHEN THOUSANDS OF YEARLINGS AND YOUNG, NON-BREEDING ADULTS CONGREGATE ON THE BEACHES TO SHED THEIR OLD FEATHERS. BY THE END OF THE MONTH MANY HAVE EXCHANGED THEIR OLD SHABBY COATS FOR SHINY, LAUNDERED TUXEDOS. THE FLEDGLINGS, ONLY THREE MONTHS OLD, HAVE MOLTED INTO THEIR JUVENILE COATS AND CONFIDENTLY MARCH TO THE SEA FOR THEIR FIRST ANNUAL MIGRATION. IN MARCH, AFTER THE LAST CHICKS HAVE FLEDGED, IT IS THE BREEDING ADULT'S TURN TO ACQUIRE A NEW SUIT. AS AUTUMN BEARS DOWN WITH ITS CHILLY WINDS, THE LAST MAGELLANIC PENGUINS PREPARE TO LEAVE THE SHORES. BY MID-APRIL, MOST HAVE COMPLETED THEIR MOLT AND BY THE END OF THE MONTH, EVEN THE MOST DIE-HARD RESIDENTS DESERT THE COLONY FOR THEIR NORTHERN WINTERING GROUNDS.

Right: YEARLING AND SUBADULT PENGUINS ALL MOLT TOGETHER ON THE BEACHES. BREEDING ADULTS ARE THE LAST PENGUINS TO MOLT AT PUNTA TOMBO AND REMAIN NEXT TO THEIR HOME BURROW.

predators, such as sharks and orcas, or overcoming temporary food shortages. Man-made perils, which they were never designed to encounter or withstand, are becoming an ever increasing threat.

Penguins spend much time preening themselves. To be impermeable, feathers must be aligned and kept smooth and clean. The preen gland, at the base of the tail, produces a special secretion, which the penguins spread over their feathers to make them waterproof.

Penguins are particularly vulnerable to oil slicks at sea. Living at the interface of water and air, they cannot simply fly over a slick as aerial birds do, and inevitably become soiled. Fouled feathers lose their insulation, which leads to hypothermia. As they try to clean themselves, the penguins ingest the petroleum, which causes gastric problems and a type of anemia. Oil-soaked penguins usually return to shore, where they slowly starve to death.

In 1987, petroleum was found on the feathers of 66 percent of the Tombo penguins. In 1991, an estimated 18,000 penguins succumbed to an unidentified spill. Scientist believe that it is not the rare, accidental oil spills, but chronic oil pollution that is seriously affecting the penguin population. The main cause for this contamination is the illegal cleansing of polluted ballast tanks by oil tankers and other ships at sea. Unfortunately, Punta Tombo lies along a main tanker route, used in the transport of crude oil from

Opposite: *During the hot summer months, Punta Tombo's beaches are filled with penguins. They come and go continuously between their burrows and the ocean, and during the morning and evening rush hours, thousands take to the water to escape the midday heat.*

Right: *Oil-covered penguins are a common sight along Patagonia's coasts. During their biannual migration between Punta Tombo and their northern feeding grounds, an estimated 10 percent of the penguins die after they encounter petroleum slicks on the way. No longer insulated against the cold southern currents, they are forced to come ashore, where they slowly starve to death. Illegal dumping of oily ballast water by tankers at sea has become the major cause of death among adult penguins.*

Comodoro Rivadavia, south of the colony, north to refineries at Bahía Blanca and Buenos Aires.

Every year, an estimated 20,000 adults and 22,000 juveniles die as they encounter petroleum along their migratory route. Over consecutive breeding cycles this abnormal mortality has become one of the main contributing factors for the decline in penguin numbers. Between October 1987 and October 1997, the breeding population of penguins at Punta Tombo declined by 16 percent.

The building of a new offshore oil rig in the Gulf of San Jorge, south of Punta Tombo, only increases the risks. The tragedy is that badly maintained drilling stations at sea, runoffs from oil wells on land, and the illegal washing of dirty ballast tanks, could all be prevented by stricter enforcement of existing laws.

While oil is the major cause of death among adult penguins, the major cause of chick death is starvation. Patagonia's penguins and Argentina's fishery compete for the same catches of anchovies, squid, shrimp, and hake. Although the latter three species have long been declared overfished, the industry continues to expand, and the South Atlantic fishery is now the fastest growing in the world. Just off Punta Tombo, local fishing boats work side by side with large commercial factory ships to catch dwindling harvests of fish and crustaceans. At the nearby colony, penguin parents have to travel farther out to sea and stay longer before they can catch food for their young, and inexperienced fledglings are more likely to starve on their first excursion out.

Ever more and ever larger boats make a penguin's life even more hazardous. The threats are manifold, and even those birds that have successfully circumnavigated oil slicks, survived food shortages, and migrated thousands of miles to their northern feeding grounds, are far from safe: a further 6 percent will drown trapped in fishing nets off the coasts of Brazil.

Hope for a Brighter Future

In order to help the penguins feed themselves and their offspring during the breeding season, environmental groups have been pressuring the government to establish a marine preserve around Punta Tombo similar to the one that protects right whales at the Gulf of San José. In 1996, large factory boats were finally prohibited from the vicinity of Punta Tombo. It may not have been coincidental that 1996 was also the most successful penguin breeding season in fourteen years.

True respite for the Magellanic penguin may come from an unexpected direction: ecotourism. In 1997 alone, Punta Tombo received over 50,000 visitors, while 100,000 people visited the Valdés Peninsula. Patagonian tourism now generates more than $50 million a year for Argentina. The tourists stay on designated trails and viewing areas and appear to have no ill effect on the penguins, since birds close to the trails quickly become accustomed to seeing humans around them.

If environmental organizations cannot press the

THREATENED BY OVER-FISHING, OIL-SLICKS, AND ENTANGLEMENT IN FISHING NETS, THE MAGELLANIC PENGUIN'S FUTURE IS FAR FROM CERTAIN, AND MORE THAN EVER DEPENDENT ON PROTECTIVE LEGISLATION THAT REACHES BEYOND ITS TERRESTRIAL BREEDING SITES, TO ITS MARINE ENVIRONMENT.

government to enforce tougher legislation, ecotourism eventually might. As the popularity of the little tuxedoed Magellanic penguin rises, together with its importance as a source of economic income, tougher legislation will hopefully follow suit. Dead penguins on the beach are, after all, bad propaganda for a world-renowned wildlife gem in a province and country that prides itself on its natural diversity and beauty.

There has been an encouraging precedent for the influence of public opinion upon government plans. In 1982, a Japanese company, Hinode S.A., sought a concession to harvest first 40,000 and eventually 400,000 penguins a year as a source of meat, oil, and high-fashion gloves. But the Argentine public, charmed by the little birds, grew indignant and outraged at the prospect of such wholesale killing. Public demonstrations managed to change the outlook of the military government, which outlawed the killing of penguins altogether. After centuries of having been salted, pickled, and smoked for food; skinned for leather; and boiled for oil; the Magellanic penguin was finally protected.

Southern Giant Petrel (MACRONECTES GIGANTEUS)

The southern giant petrel's true home lies in the circumpolar regions of the southern hemisphere. Very occasionally however, some birds wander north into more tropical zones. Although southern giant petrels feed on krill, squid, and anchovies, a large part of their diet consists of carrion from penguin colonies and seal and sea lion rookeries. They are often present around marine mammal colonies, especially during the pupping season when they scavenge on dead animals and afterbirths. They usually feed on penguin eggs and young, weak, chicks, though occasionally they will use their powerful hooked bills to kill a healthy adult. Stranded whales are a special feast. In 1985, some eighty petrels spent several weeks feeding on a whale that had stranded at Caleta Valdés. Like vultures, groups of petrels converged to feed communally on the enormous carcass, consuming large amounts of blubber until they were so gorged they could barely fly.

Left: GIANT PETRELS TEND TO BREED ON REMOTE OCEANIC ISLANDS, AS FAR SOUTH AS ANTARCTICA, BUT SCATTERED BREEDING COLONIES CAN BE FOUND ALONG PATAGONIA'S CHUBUT COAST.

Above and opposite: SOUTHERN GIANT PETRELS ARE PARTICULARLY ACTIVE IN ROUGH WEATHER. IN THE PAST, MARINERS CONSIDERED THIS LARGE, GRAYISH BIRD AN UNWELCOME HARBINGER OF STORMS. ON WINDY DAYS, THE GIANT PETREL IS A SPECTACLE. FLYING EXTREMELY LOW ACROSS THE SEA, THE TIPS OF ITS SIX-FOOT WINGSPAN ALMOST BRUSHING THE WATER'S SURFACE, THE PETREL WILL AT TIMES COMPLETELY DISAPPEAR BEHIND WALLS OF SPRAY, MAGICALLY GLIDING AWAY JUST AN INSTANT BEFORE A GIANT WAVE WASHES OVER IT.

Chubut Steamer Duck (TACHYERES LEUCOCEPHALUS)

The Chubut, or white-headed, steamer duck is a large marine duck incapable of sustained flight, although it certainly appears to try. In the face of danger, or when defending their territory, steamer ducks charge across the surface of the water, kicking violently and beating their wings like the paddles of an old steamer. The Chubut steamer duck may, however, spring several feet out of the water to land on rocks and is capable of short bursts of flight, which usually end with a splash landing on the sea. Of the three species of steamer ducks in Argentina, the Chubut is the only one to inhabit the Valdés Peninsula and Punta Tombo. In a landmark event in ornithology, the Chubut steamer duck was officially designated a distinct species in 1981, becoming the first new species of wildfowl to be discovered since 1917.

Opposite and left: THE CHUBUT STEAMER DUCK NESTS CLOSE TO SHORE, USUALLY UNDER THE COVER OF BUSHES OR LOW TREES. DURING THE AUSTRAL SPRING, THE FEMALE LAYS FIVE TO NINE IVORY-COLORED EGGS, WHICH SHE INCUBATES ON HER OWN. WHEN SHE LEAVES THE NEST TO FEED, SHE USUALLY COVERS HER EGGS WITH DOWN TO CONCEAL THEM AND KEEP THEM WARM. STEAMER DUCK CHICKS CAN SWIM AND FEED THEMSELVES SHORTLY AFTER HATCHING, BUT THEY CONTINUE TO RELY ON THE PROTECTION OF THEIR PARENTS, UNTIL THEY REACH INDEPENDENCE AT ABOUT SIXTEEN WEEKS OF AGE.

Above: THIS BIRD IS A MALE, WITH A CHARACTERISTIC YELLOW-ORANGE BILL AND GRAY HEAD, WHILE THE FEMALES OF THIS SPECIES HAVE A GRAYISH BILL AND BROWN HEAD. MALES ARE LARGER AND MORE ROBUST THAN FEMALES, ALTHOUGH THEY HAVE PROPORTIONATELY SHORTER WINGS. THE STEAMER DUCK IS HIGHLY TERRITORIAL DURING THE BREEDING SEASON AND IN SOME CASES, MALES HAVE BEEN KNOWN TO INFLICT SERIOUS INJURIES ON RIVALS.

King Cormorant *(Phalacrocorax albiventer)*

The king cormorant, or king shag *(Phalacrocorax albiventer)*, can be found from the Valdés Peninsula south to the Cape Horn area. A similar species, the blue-eyed cormorant *(Phalacrocorax atriceps)*, has a more southern distribution, ranging from the province of Santa Cruz, all the way south to the Antarctic Peninsula.

Courtship rituals begin in October and include circle-flying, wing-waving, head-wagging, and mutual preening. During the breeding season its golden nasal caruncles, the fleshy appendages above its bill, turn deep orange and it develops a recurved crest on the forehead that fades by the time the first egg is laid.

King cormorants nest on bulky cones made mostly of seaweed cemented with guano. During the nesting season, the male gathers seaweed, which the female weaves into nests with quivering motions of her bill. Both parents share the duty of incubating their clutch of three eggs and of brooding their chicks. Chicks hatch naked and do not fledge until they are seven weeks old. Although king cormorants return annually to the same nest site, they do not always mate with the same partner. Males tend to stay with the same nest, while females will settle with a new partner nearby.

Opposite: THE KING CORMORANT BREEDS COLONIALLY ON RELATIVELY FLAT TERRI-TORY, SUCH AS LOW SEA CLIFFS AND PROMONTORIES, AND SOMETIMES ALONG-SIDE PENGUINS, AS AT PUNTA TOMBO. IT IS A GREGARIOUS BIRD, AND LARGE FLOCKS OF A HUNDRED OR MORE BIRDS ARE A COMMON SIGHT ALONG THE PENINSULA'S SHORES.

Above: THE KING CORMORANT DIVES AND CHASES ITS PREY UNDERWATER, FEEDING ON FISH, SQUID, CRUSTACEANS, AND BOTTOM-DWELLING INVERTEBRATES. BUT ITS PLUMAGE IS NOT AS WATERPROOF AS THAT OF OTHER AQUATIC BIRDS AND COR-MORANTS CAN OFTEN BE SEEN SPREADING THEIR WINGS TO DRY THEIR FEATHERS IN THE WIND.

Rock Cormorant *(Phalacrocorax magellanicus)*

Above: A rock cormorant carries sea-weed back to its nest.

Opposite: Chalky deposits of dried guano mark the nest sites of small rock cormorant colonies along the peninsula's sandstone cliffs. The cormorants arrive in their breeding areas along the peninsula's coast during the month of August. Between the last week of October and the first week of December they lay two eggs, which begin to hatch in the third week of November. About half of the chicks survive to fledging.

The rock cormorant, or rock shag, is named for its habit of nesting precariously on exposed cliff ledges. It has reddish facial skin that turns a deep brick-red during the breeding season. Juvenile rock cormorants, which are dull brown, look similar to the brown-black olivaceous cormorant.

Black-Browed Albatross (DIOMEDEA MELANOPHRYS)

Brown-Hooded Gull (LARUS MACULIPENNIS)

The black-browed albatross's distinctive, sinuous brows look like Japanese ink strokes. A bird of the open sea, it spends most of its life gracefully soaring the southern ocean on long, outstretched wings.

In the peninsula's waters black-browed albatrosses can be found feeding on swarms of anchovies, alongside giant petrels, gulls, and dusky dolphins, but they are only ever seen when there is a full-blown gale, for albatrosses are creatures of the wind. Master dynamic soarers, they rarely need to flap their slender wings, which can span over eight feet (almost 2.5 m). Riding air currents that rise up from the sea, they take advantage of different wind speeds at different altitudes. The birds use strong upcurrents to gain height, swing out of the wind to plummet between the waves, point upwind to slow down, and off-wind to speed up. Most at home in the windy latitudes known as the "roaring forties," "furious fifties," and "screaming sixties," they are stranded on calm days, and are forced to sit on the surface and wait until the weather changes.

THE BROWN-HOODED GULL RANGES FROM TIERRA DEL FUEGO NORTH TO VALDIVIA IN CHILE ON THE PACIFIC COAST, AND TO URUGUAY ON THE ATLANTIC COAST, ALTHOUGH SOME BIRDS MIGRATE UP TO BRAZIL DURING THE WINTER MONTHS. DURING THE BREEDING SEASON, WHICH BEGINS IN OCTOBER, IT DEVELOPS A WHITE, CRESCENT-SHAPED EYE RING AND CHARAC-TERISTIC CHOCOLATE-BROWN HOOD. BROWN-HOODED GULLS ARE COMMON ALONG PATAGONIA'S COAST, WHERE THEY SCAVENGE FOR MOLLUSKS AND CRUSTACEANS ALONG THE TIDELINE, BUT THEY NEST ON FRESHWATER LAKES FARTHER INLAND. LIKE THE MORE NUMEROUS KELP GULLS, THEY BOLDLY RIP PIECES OF SKIN OFF THE BACKS OF SOUTHERN RIGHT WHALES.

IMMATURE ALBATROSSES MAY CIRCLE THE WORLD SEVERAL TIMES WITHOUT TOUCH-ING SOLID GROUND. IN THEIR SIXTH YEAR, HOWEVER, THEY TOUCH DOWN ON A SUB-ANTARCTIC ISLAND TO BREED. IT MAY TAKE ANOTHER TWO OR THREE YEARS BEFORE THEY ARE ABLE TO MATE SUCCESSFULLY, BUT WHEN THEY DO, IT IS FOR LIFE. BLACK-BROWED ALBATROSSES MAY LIVE UP TO FIFTY YEARS, AND A BREEDING COUPLE WILL RETURN TO THE SAME NEST SITE YEAR AFTER YEAR.

Oystercatchers

Above: LIKE ALL OYSTERCATCHERS, THE AMERICAN OYSTERCATCHER (HAEMATOPUS PALLIATUS) USES ITS ELONGATED BEAK TO PROBE FOR SMALL MUSSELS AND OTHER MARINE MOLLUSKS. IT TENDS TO MOVE IN PAIRS AND HAS A STRIDENT, HIGH-PITCHED FLIGHT CALL. IT NESTS ON OPEN GROUND, AMID THE DISGUISE OF PEBBLES, SHELLS, AND PLANT MATERIAL. WHEN APPROACHED, AN INCUBATING BIRD WILL USUALLY LEAVE THE NEST AND ALLOW THE NATURAL CAM-OUFLAGE OF THE EGGS TO DO ITS WORK. DURING THE WINTER MONTHS THE AMERICAN OYSTERCATCHER MIGRATES NORTH TO MORE HOSPITABLE CLIMATES.

Right: THIS MAGELLANIC OYSTERCATCHER STRIKES A TYPICAL DISPLAY POSE USED DURING COURTSHIP AND TERRITORIAL DEFENSE. DURING THE BREEDING SEASON, MAGELLANIC OYSTERCATCHER PAIRS CAN BE SEEN PARTICIPATING IN RITUALIZED DIS-PLAYS, WITH BOTH BIRDS CALLING OUT SIMULTANEOUSLY WHILE TIPPING FORWARD AND BACKWARD LIKE SEESAWS, AND THEN RUNNING IN UNISON DOWN THE BEACH. ITS NEST IS A MERE SCRAPE IN THE GROUND, USUALLY ON OPEN TERRAIN, WHICH THE OYSTERCATCHER DEFENDS WITH VEHE-MENCE.

Opposite: THE MAGELLANIC OYSTER-CATCHER (HAEMATOPUS LEUCOPODUS) INHABITS SOUTH AMERICA'S EXTREME SOUTH. IT LIVES IN COASTAL AREAS, WHERE IT FEEDS ON WORMS, MUSSELS, LIMPETS, AND SMALL CRABS. SOME BIRDS, HOWEVER, MOVE INLAND TO BREED DURING THE WARMER MONTHS OF THE YEAR, AND CAN BE FOUND IN MEADOWS AND ANDEAN VALLEYS.

Black-Crowned Night Heron (Nycticorax nycticorax)

Left: Between October and December, the peninsula's black-crowned night herons lay three to five bluish-gray eggs at two-day intervals, and the eggs hatch over a span of six to eight days. They nest in colonies at Isla de Los Pájaros, or singly, under the cover of cliffs, choosing bushes and low trees along the banks of Caleta Valdés, which they sometimes share with brooding steamer ducks and penguins. Breeding pairs affectionately rub bills and participate in the ritualized preening of each other's plumage. Males establish territories, which they defend by snapping and hissing loudly while fluffing their feathers. When they have chicks to feed, the parents will also fish during the day.

Opposite: One-year-old birds have orange eyes and are gray-brown in coloring with light buff spots and streaks. They do not attain full adult plumage until they are in their fourth year. Adult birds have crimson eyes and a characteristic blue-black cap and back. Their wings and tail are gray and their underparts creamy white.

Black-crowned night herons live up to their name: they spend their days roosting in bushes and trees, and come out at night, feeding mainly at dawn and dusk. Their Spanish name, *garza bruja,* or "witch heron," stems from their haunting, croaking call when flying in the pitch black night. Night herons are com- mon in tidal creeks, coastal estuaries, and lagoons, where they take advantage of the tidal flow to feed on aquatic insects, larvae, fish and crustaceans in the shallows or in rock pools. They fish by walking slowly through the water, and unlike other herons, will swim and dive to catch their dinner.

Upland Goose (CHLOEPHAGA PICTA)

Opposite: During the summer months, upland geese breed in wet valleys around ponds and lakes. In the autumn they form large flocks and migrate to spend the winter months on the vast, green pampas of the north, where they descend in droves to feed on tender winter wheat. Considered serious agricultural pests, they are often shot by farmers.

During their annual migration, flocks of upland geese settle for weeks at the Valdés Peninsula before continuing their journey. As in this picture, upland geese often travel in conjunction with ashy-headed geese (Chloephaga poliocephala), which apart from their distinctive ash-gray head and paler flanks, can look similar to female upland geese.

Left and above: The upland, or Magellan, goose belongs to the group known as sheldgeese. Essentially terrestrial birds, they are abundant in the Andes, but despite a strong preference for freshwater, can also be found along Patagonia's coast, where they can be seen both on land and swimming at sea. Male and female upland geese look strikingly different. Males are mostly white except for their back and wings, which are gray with black bars. The yellow-legged females have a rusty-brown head, neck, and breast with brown, black, and white flanks.

Swans

THE BLACK-NECKED SWAN (CYGNUS
MELANCORYPHUS) RARELY COMES ASHORE.
IT SPENDS ITS LIFE ON MARSHES AND
LAKES, AND IN FRESH- AND SALT-WATER
ESTUARIES, WHERE IT NESTS AMONG THICK
SEDGES AND RUSHES. LIKE MANY SWANS,
BLACK-NECKED SWAN PAIRS MAY BOND FOR
LIFE. THE BLACK-NECKED SWAN HAS A
BRIGHT RED FLESHY LOBE AT THE BASE OF
THE BILL THAT TENDS TO BE LARGER IN
MALES THAN IN FEMALES. IT IS A HEAVY
BIRD THAT MUST RUN AND FLAP ITS WINGS
FOR QUITE SOME TIME BEFORE IT GAINS
ENOUGH SPEED TO TAKE FLIGHT. IT CAN BE
FOUND FROM THE WETLANDS OF SOUTH-
ERN BRAZIL AND PARAGUAY TO TIERRA DEL
FUEGO, WITH THE LARGEST POPULATIONS
OCCURRING IN ARGENTINA. FOR
UNKNOWN REASONS, THOUSANDS OF
BLACK-NECKED SWANS PERISHED
THROUGHOUT PATAGONIA IN 1988 AND
1989. LIKE THE COSCOROBA SWAN, BLACK-
NECKED SWANS THAT BREED IN THE FAR
SOUTH MIGRATE NORTH IN THE WINTER.

The coscoroba swan *(Coscoroba coscoroba),* was named by South American Indians for its call, a hoarse and warbling *"cos-cor-ro-oa."* They considered it a goose, and a very tasty one. In fact, because the coscoroba swan is more goose-like than other swans, it was put into a genus of its own. Like ducks and geese, it has feathers that completely cover the facial region, while other swans have a bare, triangular patch of skin between the bill and eyes. An estimated 10,000 to 25,000 coscorobas range from Tierra del Fuego to Uruguay and southern Brazil. In winter the southernmost populations migrate north.

Ducks

Below and opposite: THE CRESTED DUCK (LOPHONETTA SPECULARIOIDES) INHABITS ANDEAN LAKES AND LAGOONS AND CAN ALSO BE FOUND ALL ALONG THE COASTS OF PATAGONIA AND TIERRA DEL FUEGO, WHERE IT PREFERS SHELTERED BAYS, SHALLOW PONDS, AND TIDELAND. PAIRS OF CRESTED DUCKS CAN BE SEEN ALONG THE SHALLOW BANKS OF CALETA VALDÉS, WHERE THEY FORAGE ON SMALL CRUSTACEANS AND MOLLUSKS. THEY HAVE A HOARSE, BARK-LIKE CALL, AND CAN BE AGGRESSIVELY TERRITORIAL DURING THE MATING SEASON WHEN THEY DISPLAY BY SWIMMING BACKWARD AT HIGH SPEEDS. DURING THE BREEDING SEASON, WHICH LASTS FROM AUGUST TO APRIL, CRESTED DUCKS OFTEN LAY EGGS TWICE. NESTS ARE CONCEALED AMONG VEGETATION CLOSE TO SHORE AND CHICKS ARE TAKEN TO THE WATER AS SOON AS THEY HATCH.

Above: THE BROWN PINTAIL (ANAS GEORGICA) CAN BE FOUND FROM TIERRA DEL FUEGO TO SOUTHERN BRAZIL. PINTAILS CAN OFTEN BE SEEN ON VALDÉS, WHERE PAIRS AND SMALL FLOCKS OF UP TO TWENTY BIRDS SETTLE ON TEMPORARY PONDS TO FEED ON SEEDS WASHED THERE BY RUNOFF FROM HEAVY RAINS. IN THE NORTHERN PART OF THEIR RANGE THEY SEEM TO BREED WHENEVER CONDITIONS ARE FAVORABLE, BUT IN PATAGONIA, THEY BREED ONLY IN SPRING.

Chilean Flamingo *(PHOENICOPTERUS CHILENSIS)*

South American Stilt *(HIMANTOPUS MELANURUS)*

The Chilean flamingo is most abundant in alkaline salt and soda lakes in the high Andes, where it breeds and feeds on microscopic blue-green algae, diatoms, and invertebrates. Of the four species of South American flamingo, the Chilean is the only one that visits the Patagonian shoreline, usually between May and September. During low tide, large flocks of Chilean flamingoes wade through the shallows around Isla de los Pájaros. Like flamenco dancers, they kick up the seabed with their long pink legs, stirring up the planktonic organisms on which they dine. They feed by hanging their heads down between their legs, separating their tiny quarry from the sand and silt with natural filters inside their oversized bills. The flamingo's color derives from pigments in its prey and intensifies during the breeding season. Flamingoes mate for life, and may live about fifty years. They lay a single egg in a conical nest of clay or mud, which they incubate for approximately twenty-eight days. For the first few weeks of their lives, flamingo young are fed on a milky secretion which is controlled by the same hormone as found in mammals, prolactin. Unlike mammals however, both male and female flamingoes are able to produce milk.

Above: A flock of South American stilts wades through the shallows at Riacho San José, using their long, slender beaks to probe for crustaceans and aquatic insects.

Opposite and pages 182–183: The Chilean flamingo looks graceful whether in flight or parading along the shore.

Part 2
The Arid Steppe

*I*n *calling up images of the past, I find that the plains of Patagonia frequently cross before my eyes; yet these plains are pronounced by all to be wretched and useless. They can be described only by negative characters; without habitations, without water, without trees, without mountains, they support only a few dwarf plants.*

Why, then, and the case is not peculiar to myself, have these arid wastes taken so firm hold of my memory?

I can scarcely analyze these feelings; but it must be partly owing to the free scope given to the imagination. The plains of Patagonia are boundless, for they are scarcely passable, and hence unknown; they bear the stamp of having thus lasted, as they are now, for ages, and there appears no limit to their duration through future time.

CHARLES DARWIN
Voyage of the Beagle, 1839

Chapter Three
Creatures of the Arid Steppe

The Valdés Peninsula is a land of extremes. Compared to the bountiful south Atlantic Ocean, which nurtures one of the richest marine faunas in the world, the barren Patagonian steppe is a harsh and unforgiving environment. On land, strange, hardy creatures scrape out the barest living in a semi-desert. Some of the indigenous animals, such as the mara or Patagonian hare *(Dolychotis patagonum)*, and the guanaco *(Lama guanicoe)*, have adapted to living on very little water. The mara's smaller cousin, the cui, or lesser cavy *(Microcavia australis)*, is a desert specialist that makes its home under clumps of thorn bushes, where it lives in small groups in a common burrow with several entrances. Cuis spend much of their time in the shade, using special runways to dart across open spaces at full speed. Their main predators on the peninsula are the Patagonian gray fox *(Dusicyon griseus)* and the red-backed hawk *(Buteo polyosoma)*. Underground burrows are the refuge of most of the peninsula's mammals—including the two indigenous armadillos, the pichi *(Zaedyus pichiy)* and the larger peludo *(Chaetophractus villosus)*; the Patagonian hog-nosed skunk *(Conepatus humboldtii)*; and the gray fox. Maras, on the other hand, use burrows only to shelter their young.

Unable to find cover on the wide open plains, the larger inhabitants of the arid steppe, such as the flightless Darwin's rhea *(Pterocnemia pennata)* and the cameloid guanaco rely on speed to flee from their predators. In the face of danger, guanacos can gallop at up to thirty-seven miles (60 km) per hour, and the rhea's long, powerful legs carry it to speeds in excess of thirty-one miles (50 km) per hour. Even the much smaller mara can leap at up to twenty-eight miles

(45 km) per hour. The mara and the guanaco have suffered from the introduction of foreign species, such as the more adaptable European hare, and intensive sheep farming which is displacing the guanaco from much of its former range. Other animals, such as the hog-nosed skunk and the gray fox, have been hunted for their pelts.

The most characteristic and best adapted bird species of the arid steppe are the Darwin's rhea, the elegant crested tinamou *(Eudromia elegans)*, and the little burrowing owl *(Athene cunicularia)*. They each have gray-brown plumage that is speckled with white, which provides the ideal camouflage for their life among the drab colors of the sparsely covered plains. When hunting from the air, the burrowing owl hovers briefly before striking, but it is equally adept at hunting on foot and spends much of its time running about nimbly on the ground looking for insects. It is

Right: The yarara ñata (Bothrops ammodytoides), a smaller relative of the rattlesnake, can grow to be twenty inches (50 cm) long. It feeds on lizards and small rodents, hiding in crevices and under bushes and shrubs. It is moderately aggressive and its venom can be fatal. It is the only venomous snake on the peninsula and the most southern residing viper in the world.

Opposite: The peninsula's plants are masters of survival: there are no long-branched trees, just low, tight bushes, such as the quilenbai and colapiche, that have evolved to withstand the constant lashing of the ceaseless wind. Tough, spiky grasses, such as the bitter coiron, grow in low clumps. Powerful roots anchor firmly into the arid soil, while rounded, cushion-like shapes preserve moisture and warmth. Many bushes and shrubs have prickly thorns or small, bristly leaves to protect themselves from grazing guanacos and sheep.

Below: Passion, lizard style.

the most terrestrial of all owls. The tinamou is also essentially a ground bird, and flies only when flushed out from the brush.

Both tinamou and rhea populations have shrunk in recent years due to the rapid loss and destruction of their habitat. The gregarious tinamous used to form large flocks of up to one hundred birds during the winter months. But their numbers have dropped due to hunting and the conversion of grassland for agri-cultural use, and small flocks of ten to fifteen birds are more common these days.

Among the peninsula's songbirds are the rufous-

THE LONG-TAILED MEADOWLARK (STURNELLA LOYCA), IS THE ONLY ONE OF ARGENTINA'S THREE MEADOWLARK SPECIES THAT CAN WITHSTAND PATAGONIA'S HARSH CLIMATE. MALES HAVE A LOUD, HARSH SONG, AND A SCARLET PATCH RUNNING FROM THE BASE OF THE BILL TO THE BELLY, WHICH IS OF AN ESPECIALLY BRILLIANT COLOR DURING THE BREEDING SEASON. THE FEMALE'S CALL IS MUCH WEAKER THAN THE MALE'S. SHE HAS A WHITE THROAT, AND HER RED PATCH IS BOTH SMALLER AND DULLER. MEADOWLARKS SPEND MUCH OF THEIR TIME ON THE GROUND SEARCHING FOR INSECTS, LARVAE, EARTHWORMS, AND OTHER INVERTEBRATES. DURING THE WINTER MONTHS THEY FORM FLOCKS OF TWENTY OR MORE BIRDS, BUT SEPARATE INTO ISOLATED PAIRS AT THE START OF THE BREEDING SEASON.

collared sparrow (Zonotrichia capensis), one of the most abundant birds in Patagonia, and the Patagonian canastero (Asthenes patagonica). The latter can be found only in northern Patagonia; it builds basket-like nests about the size of a soccer ball out of thorny twigs. The Patagonian yellow finch (Sicalis lebruni) has a loud, canary-like song. During the spring and summer months it is commonly seen along the peninsula's coast, where it nests in holes and crevices along the sandstone cliffs. The red-backed hawk (Buteo polyosoma) also nests along the peninsula's high coastal cliffs, returning to the same nest year after year. Other birds of prey that breed on the peninsula include the American kestrel (Falco sparverius), the black-chested buzzard eagle (Geranoaetus melanoleucus), the aplomado falcon (Falco femoralis), and the cinereus harrier (Circus cinereus).

THE PATAGONIAN MOCKINGBIRD (MIMUS PATAGONICUS) IS A PERMANENT RESIDENT OF THE COASTAL STEPPES. THE MOCKINGBIRD HAS A VARIED DIET, FEEDING ON INSECTS; LARVAE; AND THE FRUITS, BERRIES, AND SEEDS OF NATIVE FLORA. IT IS BEST KNOWN FOR ITS BEAUTIFUL SONG, AN ECLECTIC COLLECTION OF CHIRPS AND WHISTLES THAT NEVER SEEMS TO REPEAT ITSELF, AND WHICH IS HEARD MOSTLY AT DAYBREAK AND SUNSET. OFTEN, AS THE NAME IMPLIES, PORTIONS OF CALLS OF OTHER LOCAL BIRDS ARE COMBINED INTO THE MOCKINGBIRD'S SONG.

Guanaco (LAMA GUANICOE)

A small cousin of the camel, the guanaco is the tallest wild herbivore in Argentina, standing up to five feet, nine inches (1.75 m) tall. There is no better roof to a guanaco than the endless sky, and no safer rampart than an infinite horizon. Unlike other animals that seek shelter in forests and bushland, they arrogantly stalk the plains, fully aware that in the face of danger, their long legs can carry them away swiftly.

When the first Spanish explorers arrived in South America, millions of these graceful camelids roamed the continent all the way from the Peruvian Andes to Tierra del Fuego. An estimated thirty-five to fifty million guanacos grazed on the Patagonian pampas alone. Three hundred years later, when Charles Darwin visited Patagonia in 1833, he saw herds of up to five hundred guanacos.

For thousands of years they were a mainstay for Indian subsistence hunters, who consumed their flesh, wore their pelts as coats, and used their sinews for string. Their main natural predator was

Opposite: THE UBIQUITOUS GUANACOS ARE A SYMBOL OF PATAGONIA'S PRISTINE WILDERNESS. THEY ARE EXCELLENT SWIMMERS AND CAN BE FOUND GRAZING ON THE ISLANDS DEEP INSIDE CALETA VALDÉS, JUST AS THEY MAY BE ENJOYING A BATH IN AN ANDEAN STREAM. YET THEY CAN SURVIVE WITHOUT DRINKING FOR VERY LONG PERIODS OF TIME, DERIVING ENOUGH MOISTURE FROM THE VEGETATION THEY EAT, CAN SUBSIST ENTIRELY ON BRACKISH WATER, AND HAVE EVEN BEEN SEEN DRINKING SEAWATER.

Right: BETWEEN MID-NOVEMBER AND MARCH GUANACO FEMALES BEAR A SINGLE YOUNG THAT CAN RUN ON ITS SPINDLY LEGS WITHIN AN HOUR OF BIRTH. THEY LIVE WITH THEIR OFFSPRING IN FAMILY HERDS OF AROUND FOURTEEN INDIVIDUALS, LED BY A SINGLE DOMINANT MALE.

the puma. Today, the Indians have all but disap-peared, and the fearsome South American lion is himself battling for survival; so too, the guanacos. All three have had to face the same overwhelming threat: modern man.

By the mid-1990s, Argentina's guanacos had been displaced from half of their original range by millions of sheep. They are hunted for their wool, and also because it is mistakenly presumed they compete with livestock for grazing land and water. Hunters favor the furry, cinnamon-colored coats of chulengos, the newborn guanacos. In Argentina, the legal harvest of chulengo pelts has been a multimillion-dollar indus-try. Over 400,000 guanaco pelts were exported during the 1970s. Italian-made guanaco wool coats sold for three to five thousand dollars in the United States, and in the mid-1990s, a three-and-a-half-ounce (100 g) piece of guanaco fabric cost as much as $65. After extensive slaughtering and habitat destruction, half a million animals are thought to remain. They have been protected in Chile since 1929, in Peru since 1940, and in Bolivia since 1973. But Argentina, home to 96 percent of all guanacos, most of which live in Patagonia, did not prohibit the trade in guanaco products until 1998. By 1995, hunting quotas based on inflated estimates and illegal sport hunting had reduced the peninsula's guanaco population to less than a third of its original size.

Mara (DOLYCHOTIS PATAGONUM)

MARA PAIRS ARE INSEPARABLE, AND THEY MATE FOR LIFE. THE FEMALE LEADS THE WAY THROUGH THE DRY PATAGONIAN THORNSCRUBS, ALWAYS FOLLOWED BY HER LOYAL MATE. HIS PRIMARY ROLE IS TO WATCH OUT FOR PREDATORS WHILE SHE FEEDS AND NURSES THEIR YOUNG, AND TO DEFEND HER FROM OTHER MALES. MARA PAIRS TEND TO LIVE SOLITARY LIVES, EXCEPT FOR THE BREEDING SEASON, WHEN UP TO FIFTEEN PAIRS OF PARENTS DEPOSIT THEIR YOUNG AT COMMUNAL DENS FOR SAFETY AND WARMTH. ADULT MARAS NEVER ENTER THESE BURROWS. THEY GIVE BIRTH AND NURSE OUTSIDE, CALLING THEIR YOUNG FROM THE CRECHE WITH SOFT MATERNAL SQUEAKS. THE PARENTS RECOGNIZE THEIR OFFSPRING BY THEIR SCENT.

Maras are curious creatures, with the ears of a hare, the legs of an antelope, and a bouncing, leaping gait much like that of a kangaroo. Their white rump patches have earned them the nickname "rabbits in a miniskirt." Described by Charles Darwin as the equivalent to the European hare, they are more closely related to guinea pigs. Maras may walk, gallop, or hop like a rabbit. But when warning others, distracting a predator, or fleeing for safety, they bounce stiff-legged on all four limbs at a time, like Africa's small antelopes. Sadly, habitat destruction and the introduction of the more adaptable European hare have gradually displaced the mara from much of its original range.

Patagonian Hog-Nosed Skunk (CONEPATUS HUMBOLDTII)

Special Defense

Once I came upon a skunk and an armadillo fighting over a piece of meat. The skunk furiously squeaked and yapped in a high-pitched voice, while the armadillo, heavy and low to the ground, stood stolidly, like a miniature bulldozer. There was nothing the skunk could do, but it nevertheless kept on protesting. Suddenly the armadillo ran right over the tiny fellow, possibly trying to cut it with the serrated edges of its carapace. The skunk fell and rolled on the ground. But the fight was not yet quite over. The next thing I knew, the armadillo had a huge wet patch on its face and smelled putrid. But seemingly unperturbed, it returned to finish its meal.

Opposite: WHEN THREATENED, THE LITTLE PATAGONIAN SKUNKS STAMP THEIR FRONT FEET, RAISE THEIR TAILS HIGH INTO THE AIR, AND WALK STIFF-LEGGED. OR THEY BLUFF, STANDING ON THEIR HIND LEGS TO GIVE THE IMPRESSION THAT THEY ARE LARGER THAN THEY REALLY ARE. ONLY AS A LAST RESORT WILL THEY SPRAY THEIR FOUL-SMELLING EXCRETION, WHICH THEY AIM AT THE INTRUDER'S EYES. SKUNK SPRAY CAN CAUSE TEMPORARY BLINDNESS THAT CAN PERSIST FOR DAYS. AT THE VALDÉS PENINSULA, THE OVERPOWERING SCENT CAN EVEN BE SMELLED A HALF MILE (1 KM) OUT AT SEA.

Right: A BABY PATAGONIAN HOG-NOSED SKUNK NIBBLES ON THE BRIGHT RED BERRIES OF THE PIQUILLIN BUSH, A SEASONAL TREAT. ALTHOUGH THEY FEED MAINLY ON INSECTS, THEY ALSO EAT GRUBS AND ROOTS, WHICH THEY DIG UP WITH THEIR LONG, SHARP CLAWS. SKUNKS ARE MOSTLY NOCTURNAL. DURING THE 1970S UP TO 155,000 OF THEIR BEAUTIFULLY STRIPED SKINS WERE EXPORTED ANNUALLY.

Hairy Armadillo (CHAETOPHRACTUS VILLOSUS)

Left: THE HEAD, BACK, SIDES, AND TAIL OF THE PELUDO ARE PROTECTED BY A HORNY SHIELD, BUT ITS UNDERSIDE IS HIGHLY VULNERABLE PINK SKIN, AKIN TO THAT OF A PLUCKED CHICKEN.

Opposite: TO TOLERATE PATAGONIA'S COLD, ARID CLIMATE, THE PELUDO CONSERVES HEAT AND MOISTURE BY CHANGING ITS BODY TEMPERATURE, AND SPENDS THE COLDEST TIMES OF THE DAY UNDERGROUND.

Below: PELUDOS ARE ASTONISHINGLY FAST RUNNERS AND FREQUENTLY CHASE EACH OTHER TO CONTEST BOTH FOOD AND TERRITORY. THEIR FIGHTS ARE COMICAL AFFAIRS. THEY KICK AND SCRATCH OR COLLIDE, SCRAPING AND RASPING EACH OTHER WITH THEIR CARAPACED BODIES.

The hairy armadillo, or peludo, is named for its armor-like suit of body plates, which is covered by sparse brown hairs that protrude from between the scales. When attacked, the peludo sits tight on the ground, drawing its limbs under its carapace, or else it flees into one of the many labyrinths of its subterranean burrow, where it anchors itself with powerful claws.

Unlike its smaller and shyer cousin, the pichi *(Zaedyus pichiy),* with which it shares much of its range, the peludo does not hibernate. Both species are said to have tasty flesh and are often eaten by local sheep farmers.

Patagonian Gray Fox *(Dusicyon griseus)*

The Patagonian gray fox *(Dusicyon griseus)* is a small, slender cousin of the common gray fox, which roams the open spaces of the dry, semi-arid regions of eastern and southern Patagonia. Omnivorous and opportunistic, it forages on a variety of prey—insects, lizards, rodents, birds, and eggs. At the Valdés Peninsula, its favorite prey are hares, tinamous, and cuis, and it can sometimes be found trotting through penguin colonies looking for eggs and unguarded chicks. It also eats the crimson berries of the piquillin bush, and will consume carrion. The Patagonian gray fox mates for life, making its den under low shrubs or in burrows dug by maras and peludos.

PATAGONIA'S FOXES ARE HUNTED FOR THEIR PELTS THROUGHOUT THEIR RANGE. AT THE VALDÉS PENINSULA, LOCALS SNARE THEM BY LAYING A SHEEP CARCASS OVER A THORNBUSH AND SETTING A TRAP BELOW. OF THE THIRTEEN FOXES WE FED DURING THREE WINTERS, FOUR RETURNED WITH A MISSING PAW OR LEG, AND THREE DISAPPEARED.

IT IS SAID THAT OVER HALF OF THE TRAPS SET CATCH A GRAY FOX. DURING THE 1980S ARGENTINA EXPORTED SOME 100,000 SKINS PER YEAR. THERE ARE NO FIGURES FOR CHUBUT, BUT IN THE NEIGHBORING PROVINCE OF SANTA CRUZ, ABOUT 25,000 PATAGONIAN GRAY FOXES ARE KILLED ANNUALLY.

Above and opposite: Two BUSHY-TAILED JUVENILES ROMP AND PLAY IN THE AFTERNOON SUN.

Elegant Crested Tinamou (EUDROMIA ELEGANS)

As with their larger cousin, the rhea, the breeding role for tinamous is reversed: in early September, male tinamous select nesting territories, which they aggressively defend against other males. During the austral spring, two or three females form a breeding group that wanders from one male to another. The females assert their dominance by chasing and pecking at the male. Once the females select a male, they settle with him and begin to lay a communal clutch of six to twelve olive-green eggs with a brilliant, enamel-like finish, which are said to be among the most beautiful of all bird eggs. After the females have laid their clutch, they abandon the nest and wander off to settle with another male. In just one season, a single tinamou female may lay as many as thirty to thirty-five eggs in eight to ten different nests. When they are just one day old, the tinamou chicks leave the nest in search of food. They will never again return to the nest, but continue to stay close to their father, who protects them and broods them at night until they are at least two months old.

Darwin's Rhea (PTEROCNEMIA PENNATA)

Left: THE DARWIN'S RHEA BREEDS DURING THE AUSTRAL SPRING. THE MALE RHEA INCUBATES THE CLUTCH OF EGGS ALONE. FOR APPROXIMATELY FIVE WEEKS HE GETS UP ONLY ONCE A DAY FOR A BRIEF FEEDING STINT. ALTHOUGH HE BROODS EGGS FROM SEVERAL FEMALES, WHICH ARE LAID UP TO A WEEK APART, ALL CHICKS HATCH WITHIN THE SAME DAY. ONE-DAY-OLD CHICKS ALREADY FOLLOW THEIR FATHER AS HE FORAGES FOR INSECTS AND SEEDS. THEY LEARN HOW TO FEED BY MIMICKING HIS BEHAVIOR.

Opposite: AT ABOUT THREE AND A HALF FEET (1.1 M) IN HEIGHT, THE DARWIN'S RHEA IS PATAGONIA'S PETITE COUSIN OF THE AFRICAN OSTRICH. IT INHABITS ARGENTINA'S VAST STEPPES, BOTH IN PATAGONIA AND IN THE HIGH ANDES. IT HAS BEEN INTRODUCED TO TIERRA DEL FUEGO AND ALSO CAN BE FOUND IN CHILE, BOLIVIA, AND PERU. PEOPLE COLLECT RHEA EGGS FOR FOOD AND CAPTURE THE FLIGHTLESS BIRDS FOR THEIR MEAT AND FEATHERS, WHICH ARE USED TO MAKE DUSTERS. RHEAS ARE SWIFT AND HAVE BEEN KNOWN TO OUTRUN A HORSE. ARGENTINE GAUCHOS HUNT THEM ON HORSEBACK, USING THE "BOLA"—THREE ROUND STONES ON RAWHIDE CORDS, WHICH THEY WHIRL LIKE A LASSO AND RELEASE TO ENTANGLE THE FEET OF THE RUNNING BIRDS.

The lesser, or Darwin's rhea, has a unique social system, in which the roles of the sexes are reversed: the male builds the nest, incubates the eggs, and rears the young. The female's role is limited to mating with several dominant males and laying eggs. In late September, female rheas gather in small flocks of two to fifteen birds that wander across the plains in search of a suitable mate. To attract a harem of females, the male rhea must chase off competitors and perform elaborate courtship displays. They fight by grasping each other's bills and push to throw each other off balance, and display by bobbing their heads, spreading their wings, and ruffling the plumes on their head. Once a group of hens has selected a male they begin to follow him around. After a few days, the male leads his harem to a site where he builds a nest. During the following days the females cautiously approach the nest and lay their eggs close by. The male is very protective of the nest and can be quite aggressive. If he accepts a female's egg he will roll it into the nest, until he has gathered at least a dozen eggs. After laying her eggs, the female wanders off to find another male.

Birds of Prey

Below: THE AMERICAN KESTREL (FALCO SPARVERIUS) IS A SMALL FALCON THAT CAN BE FOUND THROUGHOUT SOUTH AMERICA. IT FEEDS MAINLY ON INSECTS, ALTHOUGH IT ALSO PREYS ON MICE AND, OCCASIONALLY, ON SMALL BIRDS. IT HAS A HURRIED BUT GRACEFUL FLIGHT AND CAN OFTEN BE OBSERVED HOVERING IN MID-AIR WHILE SEARCHING FOR PREY.

Right: THE RED-BACKED HAWK (BUTEO POLYOSOMA) IS A BIRD OF THE OPEN PLAINS AND THE MOST ABUNDANT RAPTOR OF THE REGION. IT PREYS ON SMALL MAMMALS AND RODENTS SUCH AS THE CUI. DESPITE ITS NAME, ONLY THE FEMALE RED-BACKED HAWK HAS A RUSTY, CHESTNUT-COLORED BACK, WHILE THE MALE'S BACK TENDS TO BE GRAYISH-BLUE. JUVENILES ARE DARK BROWN WITH BUFF MARKINGS.

Opposite: THE BLACK-CHESTED BUZZARD EAGLE (GERANOETUS MELANOLEUCAS) INHABITS WESTERN AND SOUTHERN SOUTH AMERICA'S TEMPERATE AND COOL REGIONS UP TO 9,800 FEET (3,000 M) ABOVE SEA LEVEL, AND CAN ALSO BE FOUND IN EASTERN BRAZIL. AT THE VALDÉS PENINSULA IT PREYS ON CUIS, HARES, SMALL MARAS, AND EVEN ARMADILLOS AND YOUNG FOXES. IT NESTS ON LARGE, ROCKY, PLATFORMS ON SANDSTONE CLIFFS AND IN THE FEW ISOLATED TREES THAT SURROUND THE DWELLINGS OF LOCAL SHEEP FARMERS. BLACK-CHESTED BUZZARD EAGLES ARE DYNAMIC SOARERS. THEY CAN OFTEN BE SEEN RIDING THE UPDRAFTS ALONG THE EDGE OF THE PENINSULA'S STEEP CLIFFS, GLIDING ALONG GRACEFULLY ON OUTSTRETCHED WINGS. THIS EAGLE IS A JUVENILE; ADULTS ARE SILVERY GRAY WITH A CREAMY-WHITE VENTRAL AREA AND A REMARKABLY SHORT TAIL.

Life at the End of the World

Left: AFTER MY TRIPOD WITH MY LONGEST (AND MOST EXPENSIVE) LENS WAS BLOWN OFF A CLIFF, I STOPPED PHOTOGRAPHING ON VERY WINDY DAYS. FEW DAYS, HOWEVER, ARE AS CALM AS IN THIS PICTURE, AND FEW SUBJECTS AS WILLING TO BE PHOTOGRAPHED AS THESE YEARLING ELEPHANT SEALS.

Opposite, above: PELUDOS ARE WALKING GARBAGE CANS; THEY WILL MUNCH ON ANYTHING THEY CAN FIND. WE ALWAYS HAD TO CLOSE ALL DOORS TO THE RANGER'S CABIN, FOR A PELUDO WOULD INEVITABLY RIP UP GARBAGE BAGS OR RAID THE LARDER. ONE DAY I EVEN FOUND ONE SITTING INSIDE THE REFRIGERATOR. THE POOR CREATURE WAS SO STUFFED IT COULD BARELY WALK, AND HIS FEASTING LEFT AN UNBELIEVABLE MESS.

Opposite, below: COMPARED TO ITS ANTARCTIC COUSINS, THE MAGELLANIC PENGUIN IS CONSIDERED TO BE VERY SHY, AND ONLY THOSE WITH BURROWS CLOSE TO THE TOURIST TRAIL SEEM UNDISTURBED BY THE PRESENCE OF HUMANS.

*B*elow the window of my Manhattan apartment on the twenty-seventh floor, tiny yellow cabs flow through endless concrete canyons like ants between blades of grass. For as far as I can see, buildings rise like mushrooms from an earth forged of asphalt. A leaden Hudson river, encased by cement, winds its way ponderously below double-decker bridges. What a contrast to the view from the little ranger's station perched atop a giant cliff overlooking the open Atlantic Ocean, that was my home at the Valdés Peninsula!

When I think of Patagonia, I miss the endless space, the open horizon, the vast empty plains, and the tempestuous ocean.

Two hundred and fifty people live crammed into my high-rise building—more than the human population on the entire Valdés Peninsula. My first year there, the brother of a Texan girlfriend decided to visit. But since

the only phones are in the village of Puerto Pirámide, there was no way for him to contact me. As he crossed the isthmus and entered the nature reserve, he asked a guard where he could find me. "Drive straight along this road. After about an hour and a half you will reach the water. Drive along the coast until you see a house and you will find her." He asked how he would recognize me, since he had never met me before. "Oh, she is the only woman over there," the guard answered.

Before I went to Patagonia, I had lived for nine years in the heart of London. At Valdés, I lived for two years in a house without a televison, telephone, or even a functioning radio—just a crackling solar-powered radio transceiver used by the rangers to communicate with each other. The most valuable commodity was water, which was brought once a month by a large truck. Delivery day was the only day when showers did not have to be rationed and clothes and dishes could be washed at will. Electricity was available only in the evenings, and needed to be tightly rationed, since it was produced by a field generator that ran on fuel. It used the same fuel used for the ranger's car, so there was always a trade-off between reading in the evenings or using the car during the day. Without any neighbors for miles, reading and cooking were the only pastimes available, and both were rationed by fuel and the fact that the nearest supermarket was in Puerto Madryn, a three-hour drive across bumpy roads. The stores at Puerto Pirámide, an hour from Caleta Valdés, were just an emergency alternative. Driving to Pirámide was a gamble—depending on what supplies might have been received that week— sometimes there was not much more than some old carrots, and the usual stock of bread, pasta, rice, and powdered milk. Once a month we would visit the supermarket and load up the car until the bumpers almost touched the road. We ate fresh fruit the first

week; vegetables until the second; potatoes, pasta, and rice for the rest of the time. I soon became an expert at creating new dishes from a can of anything and whatever rice or pasta was at hand. When it rained, the muddy roads were impassable for days, and more than once during wintertime we ran out of supplies and had to be rescued by a four-wheel drive vehicle.

What I remember most vividly about life on the peninsula are the wind and the dust. Day in, day out, the little cabin was pounded by the wind. If something was not bolted down and cemented in, it flew away. I spent many sleepless nights listening to the howling gales. There are no words to describe the eerie sensation of being besieged by such a tremendous force inside a little cabin in the middle of nowhere. Everything rattled, shook, and quivered, and the house would tremble as if it was being hoisted out of its foundations. Lifting everything in its path, the wind drove swirling clouds of dust across the plains like miniature tornadoes. Sometimes it was so violent that it would have been suicide to walk close to the edge of the cliffs—I had to wear ski goggles to be able to see outdoors. The sand and dust would creep into every orifice and every crease. I will never forget the flabbergasted camera technician in London who had to clean my lenses after several months at Valdés. He could not comprehend what I possibly could have done to them.

An advantage was that clouds of dust could also be a telltale sign of cars approaching in the distance. Even when they were still many miles away, we would know to expect company, and if a car broke down along the way, we were the first to find out, despite the lack of communication. Visitors were always welcome, and "mate," a bitter-tasting brew drunk communally out of a gourd, would be passed around over stories that lasted well into the night.

Peninsulanos have their own set of concerns. Their world is basic and clear. Is the road passable? How many of the newly shorn sheep died during the last cold spell? Did anyone see those tourists descend to the beach? The windmill is broken. So-and-so was really caught shooting a guanaco?

It was wonderful to get to know some of these people—like Wainul, a man of Tehuelche origin, who guards the shearing shed on the Caleta. Once a year, Wainul's shed becomes the focus of an enormous spectacle as dozens of gauchos descend upon it herding thousands of sheep. The rest of the year, Wainul sits in a chair in front of his hut, listening to the radio and drinking mate. A man of few words, one

Christmas Eve Wainul confided that he was a happy man—he had food, shelter, his horse, his mate—and for nothing in the world would he change his life.

Living at Valdés was like being in a fabulous zoo. Attracted by food from the ranger station, thirteen foxes lived in our backyard, armadillos scurried back and forth looking for scraps, and a shy, wild pampas cat would sneak around the house at night. On the beach below, an enormous elephant seal rookery stretched as far as the eye could see. One night I could have sworn I was woken up by lions roaring outside my window. Not until I descended to the beach the next morning did I realize that a tremendous battle had occurred during the night. The massive beachmaster that had solemnly ruled over a beach full of females had been displaced by a new, giant sultan, now snoring among his newly acquired harem.

During the fall of my second year at Caleta Valdés, a strange disease circulated among the skunks. Several of the bushy little fellows began losing their hair. Fearing that they would die of cold in the upcoming winter, the rangers captured a miserable-looking skunk and took it to the vet in Puerto Madryn. With just a few patches of hair left on its body, it looked more like a naked mouse, and was about half its usual size. The vet diagnosed a fungal disease and prescribed some pills, which he suggested we should hide inside a ball of butter or chicken fat.

Back at the Caleta, we began feeding the medicine to a tiny skunk with a bald head that often appeared in the vicinity of the ranger station. Within a week it began to visit for its daily ration of fat and saucer of milk. Soon it followed us inside the cabin, boldly strutting about, but always ready to lift its tail and spray if anyone came too close. That turned out to be a problem, since Zorri, as we named him, had a keen sense of smell. Despite his small size, Zorri soon learned how to open the oven door by jumping onto it, and then climbed inside. Another favorite hiding place was the garbage can, and the only way to lure him out of there was by tying food on a string, and pulling it out of the house, with Zorri in hot pursuit.

Zorri survived the winter and became a beautiful, furry adult. He continued to visit, mostly at night, scratching furiously at the door and squeaking incessantly until he was given something to nibble on. Other visitors included armadillos in the refrigerator, a pit viper in the radio room, and black widows in the larder.

During my two years on the peninsula, I never once missed the cluttered lifestyle of civilization. Watching breaching right whales over breakfast was infinitely more appealing than staring at a computer screen all day, rushing between appointments, answering phone calls, or paying bills. Away from the civilized world, there is so little one truly needs to be happy. Food, shelter, warmth, a sunny day.

To float in the water in complete trust with a whale the size of a large bus, to be brought a bunch of seaweed by a dolphin, to walk along the shore trailed by a pair of killer whales, to play with swirling sea lions, and to stand amidst a bustling penguin colony are among my most treasured memories.

Being in nature, however, is much more than that. It is about observing, looking, and listening. Nature reveals itself if you stand still and watch carefully. It is very subtle, and then all at once, when something happens, there is an incredible explosive action. But if you look closely, you will find a tinamou nestling among the bushes, a colorful lizard along the rocks, or distinguish the spout of a right whale among the whitecaps. If you do this long enough, it becomes a form of meditation. Suddenly you are running on nature's time, the timing of a tide, the cycle of a season, or the span of an animal's life. The rules of the civilized world, chronicled by clocks and calendar days, no longer apply. To contemplate nature and become part of it is a humbling experience that simply puts everything else back into perspective.

I COULD NOT BELIEVE MY EYES WHEN THESE YEARLING ELEPHANT SEALS SHUFFLED OVER TO ME AND STARTED TO NIBBLE AT MY RUCKSACK AND TO SPAR WITH ME AS THEY DO AMONG THEMSELVES. I HAD BEEN PHOTOGRAPHING ON THIS BEACH FOR MANY DAYS AND THEY MUST HAVE GOTTEN USED TO MY PRESENCE, FOR THEY ARE USUALLY AFRAID OF HUMANS, AND HAVE EVEN BEEN KNOWN TO INFLICT SERIOUS BITES WHEN PEOPLE VENTURE TOO CLOSE.

Glossary

BREACH A whale's complete leap out of the water, to finish with a splash.

CARUNCLES Fleshy, unfeathered outgrowths around the head and bill of a bird. In the swan, they are usually described as fleshy knobs.

CETACEAN The group of mammals that includes whales, dolphins, and porpoises.

FLUKE The tail of a cetacean.

GUANO The excrement of seabirds.

HAUL OUT Sea lions' and elephant seals' clamber onto a rock, beach, or sandbank.

POD A group of cetaceans. The term is used mostly in connection with orcas and other toothed cetaceans, while the term "herd" is used for a group of baleen whales, such as the right whale.

PINNIPEDS The marine mammals known as true seals (Phocidae), such as elephant seals, sea lions, and fur seals (Otariidae) and walrus (Odobenidae). The Latin name means "fin-footed."

PORPOISE A small cetacean with no, or an indistinct, beak. As a verb, to porpoise means to leap out of the water, which allows orcas, dolphins, sea lions, and penguins to breathe while swimming quickly.

ROOKERY A breeding colony of birds, penguins, and pinnipeds.

SUBADULT A juvenile elephant seal, sea lion, or right whale that has been weaned, but has not yet reached sexual maturity or its adult size. In the case of penguins, yearling birds are called juveniles, whereas young adults, over two years of age but too young to breed, are called subadults.

SPYHOP The action, mostly used when describing orcas, but also dolphins and right whales, of raising the head vertically out of the water and then sinking below, without much of a splash.

TAILLOB A whale's or dolphin's forceful slap with the fluke against the water, while most of the body remains just under the surface.

WEANER PUP Elephant seal and sea lion pups that have recently been weaned.

Selected Bibliography

General Reference Works and Field Guides

Carwardine, Mark. *Whales, Dolphins, and Porpoises.* London: Dorling Kindersley, 1995.

Harris, Graham. *A Guide to the Birds and Mammals of Coastal Patagonia.* Princeton, N.J.: Princeton University Press, 1998.

Leatherwood, S., R. Reeves. *The Sierra Club Handbook of Whales and Dolphins.* San Francisco: Sierra Club, 1983.

Lichter, Alfredo. *Tracks in the Sand, Shadows on the Sea.* Buenos Aires: Terra Nova, 1992.

Narosky, T., D. Yzurieta. *Birds of Argentina and Uruguay.* Buenos Aires: Vazquez Mazzini, 1987.

Reeves, R., B. Stewart, S. Leatherwood. *The Sierra Club Handbook of Seals and Sirenians.* San Francisco: Sierra Club, 1992.

Strange, Ian J. *A Field Guide to the Wildlife of the Falkland Islands.* London: Harper Collins, 1992.

Tell, G., I. Izaguirre, R. Quintana. *Flora y Fauna Patagonicas.* Bariloche: Ediciones Caleuche, 1997.

Venegas, Claudio. *Aves de Patagonia y Tierra del Fuego Chileno-Argentina.* Punta Arenas, Chile: Universidad de Magallanes, 1986.

Southern Right Whales

Arias, Alejandro. *Ballena Franca Austral.* Buenos Aires: Fundación Cethus, 1995.

Campagna, C., A. Lichter. *Ballenas de la Patagonia.* Buenos Aires: Emecé, 1996.

Payne, Roger. "At Home with Right Whales." *National Geographic* 149(3):322–39 (1976).

———. *Among Whales.* New York: Scribner, 1995.

Rowntree, Victoria J. "Increased Harassment of Right Whales (*Eubalaena australis*) by Kelp Gulls (*Larus dominicanus*)." *Marine Mammal Science* 14(1):99–115 (1998).

Thomas, P. O. "Life in the Nursery. The Playful Right Whale Calf." In David Macdonald, ed., *Encyclopedia of Mammals,* 236–37. New York: Facts on File, 1984.

Southern Elephant Seals

Campagna, C., B. J. Le Boeuf, M. Lewis , C. Bisioli. "Equal Investment in Male and Female Offspring in Southern Elephant Seals." *Journal of Zoology* 226:551–61 (1992).

Campagna, C., M. Lewis. "Growth and Distribution of a Southern Elephant Seal Colony." *Marine Mammal Science* 8(4):387–96 (1992).

Campagna, C., M. Lewis, R. Baldi. "Breeding Biology of Southern Elephant Seals in Patagonia." *Marine Mammals Science* 9 (1):34–47 (1993).

Campagna, C., B. J. Le Boeuf, S. B. Blackwell, D. E. Crocker, F. Quintana. "Diving Behaviour and Foraging Location of Female Southern Elephant Seals from Patagonia." *Journal of Zoology* 236:55–71 (1995).

Southern Sea Lions

Campagna, C. "The Breeding Cycle of the Southern Sea Lion *Otaria byronia*." *Marine Mammal Science* 1(3):210–18 (1985).

Campagna, C., B. Le Boeuf. "Reproductive Behaviour of Southern Sea Lions." *Behaviour* 104:233–61 (1988).

Campagna, C., B. Le Boeuf, H. L. Cappozzo. "Group Raids: A Mating Strategy of Male Southern Sea Lions." *Behaviour* 105:224–49 (1988).

———. "Pup Abduction and Infanticide in Southern Sea Lions." *Behaviour* 107:44–60 (1988).

Campagna, C., C. Bisioli, F. Quintana, F. Perez, A. Vila. "Group Breeding in Sea Lions: Pups Survive Better in Colonies." *Animal Behavior* 43:541–48 (1992).

Orcas

Campagna, Claudio, Juan Carlos López. "Sea Pandas." *Wildlife Conservation* 1/1994:45–51 (1994).

Ford, John K. B. "The Orca Channel." In Alfredo Lichter ed., *Tracks in the Sand, Shadows on the Sea,* 199–205. Buenos Aires: Terra Nova, 1992.

Knudtson, Peter. *Orca. Visions of the Killer Whale.* San Francisco: Sierra Club, 1996.

Heimlich-Boran, Sarah and James. *Killer Whales.* Still Water, Minn.: Voyageur Press, 1994.

López, Juan Carlos, Diana López. "Killer Whales (*Orcinus orca*) of Patagonia, and Their Behavior of Intentional

Stranding While Hunting Nearshore." *Journal of Mammology* 66(1):181–83 (1985).

DUSKY DOLPHINS

Würsig, Bernd. "A Dolphin's Day. Moods of the Dusky Dolphin." In David Macdonald, ed., *Encyclopedia of Mammals*, 194–95. New York: Facts on File, 1984.

MAGELLANIC PENGUINS

Boersma, Dee. "The Magellanic Penguin." *Animal Kingdom*, March/April 1986.

———. "The Magellanic Penguin." In Tony Williams, ed., *The Penguins*, 249–58. London: Oxford University Press, 1995.

———. "Marine Conservation: Protecting the Exploited Commons." *Society for Conservation Biology Newsletter* 3(4) (November 1996).

———. "Plight of the Penguins." *Wildlife Conservation* 101(1):20–27 (1997).

Carribero A, D. Perez, P. Yorio. *El Pingüino de Magallanes en Península Valdés: Actualización de su estado poblacional y monitoreo del impacto por hidrocarburos. Informe Técnico.* Puerto Madryn: Fundación Patagonia Natural, 1994.

Reid, W., D. Boersma. "Evolution of Parental Quality and Selection on Egg Size in the Magellanic Penguin." *Evolution* 44(7):1780–86(1990).

Scolaro, Alejandro. "A Model Lifetable for Magellanic Penguins (*Spheniscus magellanicus*) at Punta Tombo, Argentina." *Journal of Field Ornithology* 58(4):432–41 (1986).

ACKNOWLEDGMENTS

I am not a biologist, and my eight seasons in the wild could not begin to teach me the knowledge and wisdom that the distinguished scientists who have so generously helped me have learned through decades of work in the field. I am most grateful to the following experts who kindly took the time to share their expertise with me. Dee Boersma, the world's leading expert on Magellanic penguins, has worked at the Punta Tombo colony for the Wildlife Conservation Society since 1982; Professor Boersma generously read and commented on the draft of my penguin chapter. Claudio Campagna, of the Wildlife Conservation Society and the National Research Council of Argentina and one of the world's principal authorities on southern sea lions and elephant seals, has dedicated his life to studying these animals in the wild. Dr. Campagna provided me with many helpful and constructive suggestions on my pinniped chapters. William Conway, who recently retired as president and general director of the Wildlife Conservation Society, first visited the Valdés Peninsula in 1964, and recognized it as one of the world's great natural treasures. Under his leadership, the WCS worked with Argentine scientists and government officials to help establish the Punta Tombo and Valdés Península reserves; it also runs the "whale camp" on the Gulf of San José, and funds much of the ongoing research projects in the area. Dr. Conway's longstanding involvement with the Valdés Peninsula and Punta Tombo and his outstanding knowledge about the area's wildlife is unequalled, and I am particularly honored that he was willing to write the foreword to this book. Astrid Van Ginneken is co-principal investigator, with Ken Balcomb, at the Whale Research Center on San Juan Island, in Washington State. Dr. Van Ginneken—who can identify each of the ninety-eight individual southern resident orcas by sight and knows their life history by heart—designed the database used for killer-whale research at the Valdés Peninsula. I have never met anyone more passionate about an animal than she, and I am most grateful for her pertinent comments on the orca chapter. Graeme J. Gissing, a doctoral candidate at the University of Toronto, has been conducting a long-term study on the peninsula's elegant crested tinamou since 1994. Gissing, who is probably the world's only real expert on this little-studied bird, provided me with new, unpublished data from his research. His input on the bird texts was invaluable, especially since information on some of the species was extremely hard to come by. Peter Harrison, who has authored and illustrated over a dozen books on birds and is widely considered the world's foremost authority on seabirds, provided further insight on the bird section. Victoria Rowntree, director of the Right Whale Program at the Whale Conservation Institute in Boston, answered my long list of questions on the right whale chapter. A colleague of Roger Payne's, she has studied the Valdés right whale population for more than three decades. She maintains the catalog and database on all individually identified whales. The data cited in these pages, and most of the interpretations of animal behavior, are based on the research of these scientists and their graduate students.

I am especially grateful for the help I received from friends and locals: Juan Benegas, Dino Ramirez, Francisco Strickler, Roberto Bubas, and the peninsula's corps of rangers, without whose support this project would have been impossible. Yann Arthus-Bertrand and Andrés Bonetti very kindly allowed me to use some of their photos in this book. Hugo Barría of NATURATUR, which manages all of Chubut's nature reserves, kindly provided me with the latest statistics on tourism and whale watching. Hector Cassín of NATURATUR, my designated guide and supervisor, brilliantly juggled the difficult task of enabling me to get closer access than usual to the animals while maintaining strict conservation guidelines and making sure that the animals remained undisturbed by my presence. Finally, I would not have been able to stay for such an extended period of time inside the reserve, or even to photograph at the Valdés Peninsula and Punta Tombo, had it not been for the many official permits kindly issued to me by Nestor García, director for conservation at NATURATUR. Max zu Salm-Horstmar, a biology student at Bristol University, was my research assistant during his internship at Fundación Patagonia Natural in Puerto Madryn; he provided me with missing facts and up-to-date information while I was writing this book in distant New York.

I am lucky to have a sister-in-law like Roxane Farmanfarmaian, who despite her busy schedule as professional editor, acclaimed author, and mother, was willing to take time off to work over my manuscript. I am extremely grateful to her for helping me polish my text and for pointing out what was missing.

I am very thankful for the trust, patience, and flexibility of my publishers, Jean-Louis Larivière and Dudu von Thielmann, whose support was unwavering and whose positive spirit helped bridge even the worst of obstacles.

INDEX